YA
344.7307   McNeese, Tim.
MCN
               Regents of the
               University of
               California v.
               Bakke.

$30.00

DATE			

REGENTS OF THE UNIVERSITY OF CALIFORNIA

▬▬ v. ▬▬

BAKKE

American Education

and Affirmative Action

GREAT SUPREME COURT DECISIONS

Brown v. Board of Education
Dred Scott v. Sandford
Engel v. Vitale
Marbury v. Madison
Miranda v. Arizona
Plessy v. Ferguson
Regents of the University of California v. Bakke
Roe v. Wade

Great Supreme Court Decisions

REGENTS OF THE UNIVERSITY OF CALIFORNIA

─── V. ───

BAKKE

American Education

and Affirmative Action

Tim McNeese

CHELSEA HOUSE
P U B L I S H E R S

An imprint of Infobase Publishing

Regents of the University of California v. Bakke

Chelsea House
An imprint of Infobase Publishing
132 West 31st Street
New York, NY 10001

Library of Congress Cataloging-in-Publication Data
McNeese, Tim.
    Regents of the University of California v. Bakke : American education and
affirmative action/ Tim McNeese.
        p. cm. — (Great Supreme Court decisions)
    Includes bibliographical references and index.
    ISBN 0-7910-9260-7 (hardcover : alk. paper) 1. Bakke, Allan Paul--Tri-
als, litigation, etc.—Juvenile literature. 2. University of California (System). Regents—Trials, litigation, etc.—Juvenile literature. 3. Discrimination in medical
education—Law and legislation—United States—Juvenile literature. 4. Affirmative action programs in education—Law and legislation—United States—Juvenile literature. 5. Medical colleges—California—Admission—Juvenile literature. I. Title. II. Title: Regents of the University of California versus Bakke. III.
Series.
    KF228.B34M36 2006
    344.73'0798—dc22   2006007329

Chelsea House books are available at special discounts when purchased in
bulk quantities for businesses, associations, institutions, or sales promotions.
Please call our Special Sales Department in New York at (212) 967-8800
or (800) 322-8755.

You can find Chelsea House on the World Wide Web at
http://www.chelseahouse.com

Series design by Erika K. Arroyo
Cover design by Takeshi Takahashi

Printed in the United States of America

Bang EJB 10 9 8 7 6 5 4 3 2 1

This book is printed on acid-free paper.

All links and Web addresses were checked and verified to be correct at the time
of publication. Because of the dynamic nature of the Web, some addresses and
links may have changed since publication and may no longer be valid.

Contents

Introduction

The year was 1973. It was late in the afternoon on August 3, but the California sun was still hot, the temperature hovering near an uncomfortable 100 degrees. One consolation was that it was Friday, the end of the workweek, and, "in California, the weekends begin early."[1] For Allan Paul Bakke, however, the weekend would have to wait. He had a 100-mile trip ahead of him. Bakke, a 33-year-old aerospace engineer who worked at NASA's Ames Research Center near Stanford University, had business at another academic institution, the University of California, Davis, outside San Francisco. Bakke knew this would be an important meeting—one that could determine the future of his entire career.

The Ames facility, spread out along San Francisco Bay's southern peninsula, is an important part of the National

Aeronautics and Space Administration's research program. As one NASA official described the facility, Ames is "a college campus of ideas."[2] The space research lab complex does, in fact, look something like a college campus, with its "formal walks, circles, and lawns that connect the jumble of brick and concrete buildings."[3] That look is only on the surface, however. On closer inspection, the Ames facility is dominated by massive cylindrical barrels of steel and aluminum, which flank the brick-and-mortar buildings. These are giant testing areas filled with wind tunnels and centrifuges. It is in these futuristic-looking buildings that NASA officials, such as Bakke, test the latest in air- and spacecraft. That summer, in a dark corner of one of the Ames buildings, sat a scale model of America's first space shuttle, *Enterprise*. It was still under design and construction.

Although he worked for an important government program, Allan Bakke was ready to change careers. He longed to become a medical doctor. It was through his work at the Ames center, where NASA scientists like Bakke designed and built experimental aircraft and space vehicles, that he had decided to change his profession. At work, Bakke had regular contact with doctors. It was their job to study the latest craft designs and mock-ups and decide whether "the frail human cargo of the billion-dollar machines could endure the punishment of our most alien frontiers."[4] Their studies fascinated him; their attention fixed ultimately on humans and their limits, rather than those of machines. Bakke had worked at NASA and helped design their machines for six years. He was ready to make a change.

ENTRANCE DENIED

Allan Bakke had applied for admission to the medical program at Davis but had been rejected. Undaunted, Bakke applied a second time, and his interview with university officials was scheduled to take place in a few weeks. It was an interview that Bakke was nervous about. On this Friday afternoon, he was driving

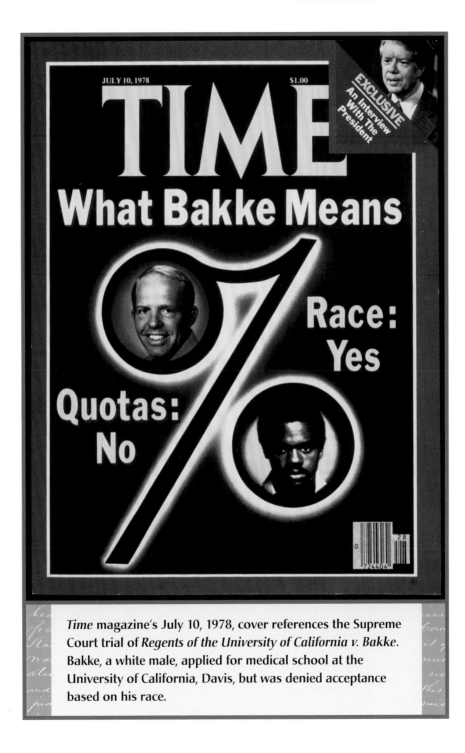

Time magazine's July 10, 1978, cover references the Supreme Court trial of *Regents of the University of California v. Bakke*. Bakke, a white male, applied for medical school at the University of California, Davis, but was denied acceptance based on his race.

up to Davis to meet with a university official to talk about his application. The meeting was not official, however. They were scheduled to meet after hours.

Even as Allan Bakke drove along the eastern fringes of San Francisco toward the university, he was mindful that his new dream of getting into medical school was still not a reality. He had, over the past two years, applied to a dozen medical schools. In 1972, he had applied to the University of Southern California and Northwestern University. Each had turned him down. The following year, Bakke had applied to University of California campuses at Davis, Los Angeles, and San Francisco, as well as Stanford University. He also applied to the University of Minnesota, the Mayo Medical School, Georgetown University, the University of Cincinnati, Bowman Gray Medical School at Wake Forest, and the University of South Dakota. He had been invited to interview at three—Stanford, Minnesota, and Mayo—but they all eventually bypassed his application. At least two schools, including the University of California, San Francisco, had explained why they would not accept him as a student. It was his age: Allan Bakke was 33 years old, older than nearly all students in American medical schools. As university admission officials put it, Bakke's age was "a negative factor."[5] Of all the factors that might keep Bakke from gaining entrance into medical school, that was one he could not control and could do nothing about.

There was another reason for Bakke being denied entrance to medical school, and again, it was one he could not control. As Bakke drove to his scheduled meeting that Friday afternoon, his car covering the miles through the arid coastal hills heading toward the trapped heat of the Sacramento Valley, someone was waiting for him on the Davis campus. This person was ready to explain, even if unofficially, why someone as intelligent as Bakke, whose academic records and tests indicated he was qualified to attend medical school, had not been accepted to the University of California campus.

Peter Storandt was an assistant to the dean of student affairs at Davis. A 30-year-old professional, Storandt had grown up in university settings; his father worked at Cornell as an admissions officer. He was a shy man of medium build, sometimes intense in his work and with others. He looked younger than his age; his clear complexion left his cheeks in a constant state of flush. Not too many years earlier, Storandt had considered attending medical school himself but had decided he "did not have the aggressive character and intense competitive spirit to pursue a premedical education."[6] Storandt had, instead, opted to study English literature.

His studies had taken him into a doctoral program at the University of Massachusetts in the late 1960s, a degree he had nearly completed when his wife became pregnant. Facing this new reality, and realizing that literature degrees don't always lead directly to jobs, Storandt left the program and moved to Detroit, where he was hired by the medical school at Wayne State University. He was not employed as a doctor, naturally, but as a counselor on the college's admissions team. Over the next few years, Storandt remained mobile in his career. He took a subsequent admissions post at the Medical College of Pennsylvania, then moved to California to take a position at Davis.

Although he had not been with the University of California for long, Storandt had already gained a reputation as a student advocate, even when it placed him at the center of controversy. Perhaps that was what had led him to agree to meet with Bakke that afternoon. He wanted the meeting to go off quietly, however. He had scheduled to meet with Bakke after classes were over for the week and the campus was nearly empty. He would be the only one still left in his office at 6 P.M., when Bakke arrived. He had information that Bakke needed—information that would explain how the university selected students for its medical school. It would prove to be information that Bakke would find disturbing.

Leaving Interstate 80, Bakke soon found the university, making "his way through the maze of roads and driveways that crosshatch the campus."[7] The temperature was cooling quickly from its afternoon high, a change typical of a northern California summer evening. He arrived at the medical school and found Storandt waiting in a green metal prefab building, one of several that composed the medical school complex. These facilities were out of date, some of them nothing more than old army barracks. The medical school at the Davis campus, was, after all, relatively new, having been established in 1968. Nearby, the new medical facilities were still under construction.

Bakke's contact with Storandt was not his first with university officials at Davis. When he first applied to the medical school, in 1971, Bakke had thought that his age might become a factor in the selection process. He had contacted an associate dean, Dr. Alexander Barry, by letter, asking Barry if his age would work against him. The dean had responded with a letter of his own, telling Bakke that there was no established age limit for applying to medical school at Davis. Barry had added, however, that the "Committee does feel that when an applicant is over 30, his age is a serious factor which must be considered. . . .The Committee believes that an older applicant must be unusually highly qualified if he is to be seriously considered for one of the limited number of places in the entering class."[8] The dean had emphasized the need for high qualifications to enter the Davis medical school.

Allan Bakke was an aerospace engineer. He had performed well on his medical school entrance exams, scoring in the ninety-seventh percentile (or in the top 3 percent) on scientific knowledge, the ninety-sixth percentile in verbal ability, and the ninety-fourth percentile in mathematics. His general knowledge score was in the seventy-second percentile. Bakke's tests were "higher than those of the average student admitted to Davis."[9] Why should age be a factor, then, in his admission? There must be something else that had caused him to be turned down by the medical school admissions committee.

A FATEFUL MEETING

Bakke found the campus building to which Storandt had directed him and was soon standing in the same room with the admissions official. The two shook hands, and Storandt offered Bakke a cup of coffee. They sat down together, and the young college official began making small talk with Bakke, trying to get to know him a little better. Later, Storandt described Bakke at their meeting as "somewhat humorless, perfectly straightforward, zealous in his approach; it was really striking; he was an extremely impressive man."[10] Despite Storandt's efforts to get to know Bakke, the aerospace engineer wanted to turn the conversation to the subject that had led him to drive so far that late afternoon. Bakke was a man in search of answers.

It would be Bakke's "straightforward" approach that would cause Storandt to offer up a trove of information about the admission practices of the Davis-based medical school. The applicant asked questions in a logical sequence, almost with a journalist's distraction, which caused Storandt to open up and tell him everything he wanted to know. The picture he painted would not please Allan Bakke.

For the class that was to begin in the fall of 1973, the school had received applications from nearly 2,500 would-be medical students. There were only 100 places in the class, however. The admissions committee proceeded to separate the submitted applications into three piles. One of those stacks was created by applicants who had checked off "yes" to the following question on Line 22 of the application form: "Applicants from economically and educationally disadvantaged backgrounds are evaluated by a special subcommittee of the admissions committee. If you wish your application to be considered by this group, check this space."[11]

Just a few years earlier, in 1968, America had experienced a difficult time of national unrest. At least a portion of that unrest was centered in an intense atmosphere of racial strife. The civil rights movement, one that began with nonviolent protests such as sit-ins and peaceful demonstrations, had evolved, and those who pressed for the resolution of racial issues were becoming more and more militant.When the civil rights leader Dr. Martin Luther King, Jr., was assassinated in the spring of 1968, urban riots rocked the nation from Los Angeles to Newark, New Jersey, as frustrated blacks expressed their anger. The long era of American racism had finally reached a breaking point, and many white Americans took steps to "correct the inequities of discrimination."[12]

It was in that spirit that, in the same year, the Association of American Medical Colleges (the AAMC) decided to recommend to medical schools across the country to "admit increased numbers of students from geographical areas, economic backgrounds and ethnic groups that are now inadequately represented."[13] In 1969, the AAMC offered a suggestion that all U.S. medical schools open up 12 percent of their first-year medical school classes to black students, beginning with the 1975–1976 school year. At least 100 schools responded positively to the proposal, including the University of California, Davis.

At Davis, the faculty established a subcommittee of admissions officers that came to be known as the Task Force. The Davis program went even further than the AAMC-suggested guidelines. In the fall of 1970, the medical school accepted 50 medical students; 8 of those were to be determined by the Task Force. Generally, the Task Force selected medical school applicants who were people of color. Later, when the entering class was raised to 100 new students, the Task Force was asked to select 16. The results were obvious. Between 1970 and 1974, the Task Force admitted 33 Hispanic Americans, 26 blacks, and one Native American to the Davis medical school. At the same time, the Task Force did not select any white students. Although part of the AAMC's suggestions had been for medical schools to select a portion of their candidates based on their low income levels, the Task Force had selected only minorities.

As Bakke and Storandt talked, the entire Davis admissions process unfurled before the aerospace engineer's eyes:

> Bakke did not believe the official description of the Task Force program sent to him by Storandt. As the engineer fired questions, Storandt gave him details: No whites had been accepted through the Task Force; the grades and test scores of minority applicants were lower than those of whites who applied; yes, Storandt understood the number of minority admissions was set at 16 for each class. . . .When the conversation ended, Bakke knew nearly as much as Storandt about the admissions procedures at Davis.[14]

After pumping the assistant dean for information and learning the truth about why he probably had not been accepted to Davis, Bakke was, for the moment, somewhat satisfied. When he and Storandt finished, he understood that his age was not the primary reason he had been denied admission. Having gained a new understanding, he left Storandt, got back in his car, and began the rest of his extended Friday evening drive—only this time, he was headed back home to his wife and children.

The night had turned foggy, and Bakke drove carefully, listening to the car radio. The news was a mixture of good and bad—more about President Nixon and the expanding Watergate scandal and the war in Cambodia, as well as a report on a new low for unemployment. Bakke was lost in his thoughts, though. He was beginning to formulate a plan concerning his dream to attend medical school. He would apply to Davis again. If he was turned down, he would speak out against the medical school's Task Force, since it was basing its decisions regarding applicants not strictly on the basis of their level of poverty, but on the basis of race. He was beginning to understand that he, a white American, had been the victim of racial discrimination. Allan Bakke's plan for future action would probably include suing at least one of the medical schools that had denied him entrance—either Stanford; the University of California, San Francisco; or the University of California, Davis. He did not know then that the case he would instigate would become one of the most significant cases concerning discrimination in American schools since *Brown v. Board of Education of Topeka,* a generation earlier. He also did not know that the case would receive an extraordinary amount of national attention.

When Bakke's case was scheduled for a hearing before the U.S. Supreme Court on October 12, 1977, tickets for the session "would be as much in demand as passes to the World Series taking place between the Yankees and the Dodgers."[15]

Discrimination in Early America

Even as the United States of America was born, its leaders set for themselves and the people they represented many high ideals, most stretching further than almost any of their day. As the 13 British colonies of North America attempted to move out from under the control of Great Britain's Parliament and King George III, the colonies united to form a country. In doing so, its leaders recognized that, as they threw off the yoke of colonialism, they had to declare the colonies they represented as independent from British authority.

JEFFERSON
AND DISCRIMINATION

The list of America's Founding Fathers (those who supported the American Revolution, the colonies' separation from Great Britain, and the framing of a new American republic) includes names readily recognized more than two centuries later—Washington, Adams, Madison, Hamilton, and Franklin. Also included among those who truly made a difference in the Revolution and the future United States was a young Virginian named Thomas Jefferson. It was Jefferson who penned the words to the Declaration of Independence, one of the truly foundational documents for the new republic. Did Jefferson really mean the words he included, though, which are quoted by many Americans today, that "all men are created equal"? Since Jefferson was a slaveowner, the question is worth asking.

The answer is generally simple. Although Thomas Jefferson believed in the words "all men are created equal," perhaps even he did not mean for them to be taken literally in every way. As a slaveholder and a Southern planter, Jefferson did not believe in the true "equality" of blacks as a race. When he wrote those otherwise stirring words, he did not intend for them to apply to blacks, nor was he "supporting black claims for freedom."* Founding Fathers such as Jefferson and John Adams (himself no slaveowner), both of whom served together on the committee that drafted the Declaration of Independence, typically distinguished between the rights for white men that they were upholding in the Declaration of Independence and the rights that blacks, especially slaves, were being denied. Jefferson and others on the Declaration committee were so certain that blacks had no legitimate claim to the rights due to whites "that they felt no need to qualify their words proclaiming universal liberty."** Thus, Jefferson was not beyond limiting the rights of blacks, and, thus, discriminating against them, even as he was contributing to the formation of a new nation founded on liberty and equality.

Jefferson the slaveholder did not believe in the equality of blacks and whites. He felt blacks to be inherently inferior. This was at a time when other whites were debating whether blacks were inferior by race or simply perceived to be inferior because they were slaves.

In his collection of observations, *Notes on Virginia*, written in the early 1780s, when the American Revolutionary War was still being fought, Jefferson expressed his doubts about the equality of blacks to whites. Although he appears to have recognized blacks as equal to whites in a "moral sense," he supported the common racist view of the eighteenth century that blacks were "inferior to the whites in the endowment both of body and mind."[***] It was this racism, after all, that allowed Jefferson to hold slaves. It was the only way "he could deal psychologically with his own sense of guilt in owning slaves."[†]

It should also be noted that, while Jefferson did not believe in the inherent equality of the races and salved his conscience by believing blacks to be inferior, he became convinced that slavery was a moral wrong. He argued against slavery by the end of the American Revolution and called for its end. He wrote during the 1780s of his belief that "the spirit of the master is abating, that of the slave is rising from the dust." He hoped for a day, publicly and privately, when America would witness "a total emancipation."[††] That day would finally arrive, but not until nearly 40 years after Thomas Jefferson's death.

[*] Quoted in Darlene Clark Hine, *The African-American Odyssey.* Upper Saddle River, NJ: Prentice-Hall, 2005, p. 104.

[**] Ibid.

[***] Quoted in Noble Cunningham, *In Pursuit of Reason: The Life of Thomas Jefferson.* Baton Rouge: Louisiana State University Press, 1987, p. 62.

[†] Ibid.

[††] Ibid., p. 63.

WORDS OF EQUALITY

Through the early summer of 1776, members of the Second Continental Congress voted to declare this new independence. To make their goals and reasons clear to all, they appointed a committee to draft, or write, a document of explanation and justification. The committee comprised such important revolutionary leaders as Benjamin Franklin, John Adams, and Thomas Jefferson. Jefferson was selected to do the writing. The result was one of the most important and foundational documents in all of American history: the Declaration of Independence. This framework in support of liberty and self-government included a deathless phrase that can be quoted by many Americans today: "We hold these Truths to be self-evident, that all men are created equal, that they are endowed by their Creator with certain unalienable rights [rights that cannot be taken away], that among these are Life, Liberty and the pursuit of Happiness." These words still stir the hearts of Americans today, as well as of many people around the world who know the taste of freedom or themselves long to become free.

The Declaration of Independence would serve as a touchstone for those who fought and otherwise defied British authority during the American Revolution. Its high ideals and intent only managed to inspire an entire generation of Americans who were willing to fight for their own freedom and that of others. As the new nation was founded, then, this concept of freedom and independence was always highly valued. Among the intentions of its creators and designers, however, the Declaration of Independence also clearly expresses a view that during much of the world's history had never been taken seriously—"that all men are created equal." Although Jefferson used the word "men" in writing the Declaration, he did not mean it to refer just to males. He was referring to all people, all "mankind." Today, writers are much more likely to use the word "humanity" or "humankind."

Throughout history, cultures and societies around the world have been built on a sentiment completely opposite to that expressed in the words of Thomas Jefferson. Some cultures and political powers believed in the superiority of some groups and the inferiority of others. Sometimes these differences were based on political or cultural differences. Other times they were based on one's religion or belief system. In many cases, the differences had to do with race or ethnicity. Whether a person belonged to one race or another sometimes determined whether he or she would be treated as an equal. Even Thomas Jefferson, the author of the Declaration of Independence, did not believe that blacks were "equal" to whites.

Despite this founding ideal of equality, throughout much of the history of the American colonies and of the United States, Americans have struggled with prejudice. Sometimes that prejudice has been directed at people because of the color of their skin. Other times, it has targeted those considered to be of a lower class. It has also been directed at the poor or foreign, or those who lack an adequate education. Although all these conditions and circumstances have led Americans to act with prejudice, no condition has been as prominent as race. Racial discrimination would help lead to the establishment of one of the most destructive institutions in American history—slavery.

EARLY AMERICAN DISCRIMINATION

Through the centuries, many Americans have struggled with racial prejudice. Generally, this prejudice has been practiced by whites against racial minorities, especially blacks. This prejudice dates back to even the earliest colonies founded by English explorers, adventurers, investors, and sea captains. It did not begin as dramatically as the prejudice would come to be held by later generations.

In 1607, after a generation of failed attempts, English settlers managed to found the first successful and permanent English colony in North America. It was established along the Atlantic coastlands that the English would call "Virginia," after their recently deceased queen, Elizabeth, known as the "Virgin Queen."

The Declaration of Independence states that all men are created equal, but that sentiment did not continue in practice. Throughout the nation's history, there have been many instances of prejudice against minority groups.

The site, established by about 100 intrepid Englishmen (no women arrived with this first group), was called Jamestown and was located along the James River. During the first decade or so, the colony remained populated by English colonists. By early 1619, however, the colony was also inhabited by those of another race. There were 32 blacks living in Jamestown by then—15 men and 17 women. History does not record how they came to be at Jamestown or how long they had even been there, only that they were "in the service of sev[er]all planters."[16] Then, in August of that same year, a Dutch ship, *Jesus of Lubeck*, arrived at Jamestown in search of trade goods. Onboard was a small "cargo" of 20 black Africans from Angola. These Angolans—17 men and 3 women—had been captured from a Portuguese slave ship that had been attacked by the Dutch vessel with help from an English ship. (These 20 Africans had been among 300 taken by the Portuguese, who had then set sail for the New Spanish city of Vera Cruz in modern-day Mexico.)

The Dutch exchanged the blacks for trade items, including food, thus introducing the practice of buying and selling Africans in British North America. Although this activity planted the seeds of what would become the slave trade in the region, the English living at Jamestown did not consider these first blacks in North America to be slaves:

> The colony's inhabitants, for two reasons, regarded the new arrivals and those black people who had been in Jamestown earlier to be unfree, but not slaves. First, unlike the Portuguese and the Spanish, the English had no law for slavery. Second . . . the Angolans . . . had been converted by the Portuguese to Christianity. According to English custom and morality in 1619, Christians could not be enslaved. So, once these individuals had worked off their purchase price, they could regain their freedom.[17]

The Angolans were introduced into Jamestown society and became servants to some of the settlement's important officials and planters, but they were not slaves. Thus, when two of these Angolans, Antoney and Isabella, married in 1623, and had a child the following year, that child was born free. Other blacks imported to the British colonies of North America experienced similar circumstances.

For more than a generation, blacks arrived in Jamestown and in the English colonies that were being established up and down the Atlantic Coast. The Dutch West India Company brought a shipload of Africans to the Dutch colony of New Amsterdam (the colony would later become New York) in 1626. These blacks labored as servants for several years but gained their freedom in 1644, after working off the cost of their ocean passage to America.

At first, the number of black workers imported from Africa remained small and insignificant. Even 30 years after the Dutch arrived with 20 Africans, there were only about 300 blacks in Virginia, compared with a total non–Native American population throughout the colony of nearly 19,000! The vast majority of these early black arrivals were considered indentured servants (slavery remained undefined and illegal in British North America).

An indentured servant could be someone of any race (the majority in the English colonies were, of course, white) who came to America but did not have the money to either pay for his or her ship passage or purchase land once he or she arrived. Such immigrants were hired out to someone willing to pay their passage, and they were required to serve an indenture, a specified period of time, often five to seven years, to pay off their debt. After that, the contract was satisfied, and the indentured servant was given his or her "freedom dues" and allowed to leave to seek his or her own future. Indentured servants, whether black or white, "could expect eventually to leave their masters and seek their fortunes as free persons."[18] At least for a while in early American history, blacks were able to enjoy a status not much different from whites. They were allowed to own property and hold public office. Some even worked their own servants, some of whom were white. It appears, then, that, during the first 40 years of English settlement in North America, blacks "seemed to enjoy a status similar to their white counterparts."[19] Unfortunately, this did not remain the case.

CREATING A SYSTEM OF DISCRIMINATION

Between 1640 and the turn of the eighteenth century, everything changed between the black and white races in English America. During those years, the number of poor whites who immigrated to America as indentured servants remained high. White indentured servants outnumbered black servants three to one. By 1700, however, the number of new whites coming to America in that way dropped drastically. Still needing a viable work force, the English turned increasingly to blacks to fill that role. Many of these black laborers were no longer being used as indentured servants, though. They were being purchased as slaves. What brought about this important change? Simply, the English had come to view slavery differently. To compete with other European powers involved in the lucrative Caribbean sugar trade, the English began using African slaves as their work force. Also, by 1700, the English had gained control of much of the trans-Atlantic slave trade. All these factors caused slavery to develop in the English colonies of North America.

With the advancement of slavery came the advancement of racial discrimination. Not only were blacks imported as slaves, but they were also treated differently than white workers. By the 1640s, colonial laws, especially in the Southern colonies, were limiting the privileges of black workers by denying them the right to own a gun. Laws were passed stating blacks were not to marry whites. Church of England leaders preached that blacks should be denied Christianity. During that same decade, Tidewater courts in Virginia and Maryland made it legal for "persons of African descent to serve their master for life rather than for a set term."[20] By the 1660s, the Virginia House of Burgesses passed a law designating the children of slave women as slaves. (This discriminatory move ran against English common law, which stated that the father's status, as slave or free, determined the status of a child.) Other laws passed in the 1660s were written to discriminate against blacks and were based on the assumption that slavery was "the natural condition of black people."[21] All these laws helped to create and strengthen an abiding sense among whites that slavery was a legitimate way of limiting the lives of blacks. Such attitudes only increased the level of racism and discrimination. The practice of legalized "slavery-for-life" was in place by the latter decades of the seventeenth century, and the system of slavery in America would remain the law of the land until the American Civil War, 200 years later.

For those unfortunate blacks who were removed from their homes in Africa and brought to America to serve others for life, their world was turned upside down. The miseries began with the forced separation from their families and other familiars. They were taken as captives and forced to march to coastal holding facilities until they could be sold onto European ships bound for America and the Caribbean. The entire process of enslavement was little more than a psychological terror. Blacks were rounded up, stripped, branded and forced into ship holds by the hundreds. What followed was a two-month voyage of despair and misery. The slaves were crowded below decks with little sanitation, bad food, and foul-smelling air. Some turned to suicide, choosing to starve themselves or jump overboard to drown or be eaten by sharks. Some poor slave victims simply went mad.

Once they were brought to the New World, their lives were marked by extremely hard work and constant discrimination. They were sometimes treated with little more regard than animals, and such comparisons were even made by their white owners. One English slave owner noted of a new arrival from Africa that he could be trained to obey, but that the process required "more hard Discipline than a young Spaniel."[22]

SLAVE DISCRIMINATION AND THE REVOLUTION

Throughout the early 1700s, slavery continued to develop and even thrive. The numbers of slaves surged as the institution became so commonplace that some Southern colonies were home to more black slaves than whites. By 1790, about 250,000 blacks had been imported into the British colonies of North America. Even as early as 1750, though, the number of slaves in America had topped the 700,000 mark. By far, the majority of those slaves were held in Southern colonies, from Maryland to Georgia. Only about 40,000 lived in the Middle colonies (Pennsylvania, New York, Delaware, and New Jersey) and New England (New Hampshire, Massachusetts, Connecticut, and Rhode Island.) Slavery was, indeed, part of a Southern way of life.

The discovery of new lands and the control of new territories brought about a need for workers to help harvest resources. Much of this work went to slaves who were bought by rich landowners. This engraving, circa 1595, depicts African slaves harvesting sugar cane on the island of Hispaniola, present-day Haiti.

By the 1770s and 1780s, political events in America would bring about significant changes for the institution of slavery. From 1775 until 1783, American colonists struggled to gain their independence from Great Britain. This independent-minded spirit led some to question the institution of slavery. As one patriot leader, James Otis, would observe: "The Colonists are by law of Nature free born as indeed all men are, white or black. . . . Does it follow that 'tis right to enslave a man because he is black?"[23] Another revolutionary leader, Benjamin Rush, who would sign the Declaration of Independence (written by

Jefferson during this period), expressed the same sentiment, trying to convince his fellow patriots that "the plant of liberty is of so tender a nature, that it cannot thrive long in the neighborhood of slavery."[24] Many blacks had participated in the war, fighting on the side of the patriots. Throughout this extraordinary period of change, some Americans began to change their view of blacks in general and of slavery specifically.

When the Revolutionary War ended, Americans emerged free from British control, even as they established their new nation, the United States of America. The prevailing spirit that had led Americans in their struggle against the British was their intense desire to live freely, to support the cause of liberty. Throughout those years—with constant references to freedom, independence, personal liberty, and the natural rights of humans everywhere—some Americans saw for the first time the damaging effects of slavery on its victims. They understood that nothing in America was based on a greater denial of freedom than slavery. As a result, several new states (former colonies) passed laws in opposition to slavery and the slave trade. By 1784, every Northern state except for New York and New Jersey had passed new laws requiring the immediate end of slavery or a plan to phase out slavery over a number of years. Free blacks across the North dramatically increased in numbers. Their numbers even increased in some Southern states. In 1782, the number of free blacks in Virginia numbered no more than 2,000. Eight years later, their numbers had increased to 13,000. By 1810, they numbered more than 30,000. Yet slavery did not lose its position of dominance across the South following the Revolutionary War and would not until the coming of another American war—the Civil War.

Despite the significant strides taken against slavery, for many of America's blacks, the spirit of discrimination and racism remained a constant thorn in their side. A new form of racism began to spread. Since many whites had justified slavery for years on the assumption that blacks were inferior, this same argument was used to justify keeping the new nation's blacks from enjoying the fruits of full citizenship. Racist whites claimed that "black people were unsuited for freedom or citizenship."[25] This view gave them an out regarding the words written by Thomas Jefferson—"all men are created equal." Because blacks were obviously not the equals of whites, it was believed, then the sentiment and ideal expressed in the Declaration of Independence surely must not apply to them.

These attitudes led to a new form of discrimination against blacks, even in the Northern states that had only recently outlawed the institution of slavery. In 1790, Congress (which had just come into existence under the newly ratified U.S. Constitution) passed a law that restricted the granting of naturalized citizenship to "any alien, being a white person."[26] In 1792, Congress again struck a blow against blacks by restricting membership in state militias to "each and every free, able-bodied white male citizen."[27] There were many other such laws passed during these years, especially at the state level. Blacks were sometimes forced to establish their own schools, because white leaders did not allow black children to attend public schools.

As the nineteenth century approached, the hope among blacks in America that the immediate future might bring new possibilities was quietly crushed. Slavery, despite the American Revolution and its calls for liberty and equality, would continue throughout the South. Discrimination would continue to thrive, even in a newly liberated America.

EQUAL·JUSTICE·UNDER·LAW·

2

New Targets of Discrimination

R acism and discrimination were never out of fashion in
America throughout the nineteenth century. Many different ethnic and racial groups became targets, and government
officials and others in positions of authority typically did little
to stop such activities or to curb such sentiments. European
immigrants were often the focus of discriminatory policies.
Sometimes, these newly arrived Europeans were treated with
disrespect, prejudice, and even violence.

THE UNWANTED IRISH

Irish immigration to America began as early as the 1600s. A
significant number of Irish came to the 13 British colonies in

the decades before the American Revolution. The first national census following the establishment of the United States was made in 1790. According to that census, nearly 45,000 Americans had been born in Ireland and immigrated across the Atlantic at some earlier date. In addition, historians estimate that another 150,000 people descended from the Irish were also living in the United States. The total population at the time was 4 million. Other historians consider these estimates to be low, contending instead that, in 1776, approximately one of every three Americans were Irish or of Irish ancestry.

Some of these numbers remain in dispute. Despite continuous immigration from Ireland during the 1600s and 1700s, though, it cannot be disputed that most arrived in the 1800s. This immigration began at the opening of the century, when the United States, as a nation, had been established for only a few decades. Then, from 1800 through 1830, the numbers of Irish coming to America began to increase—there were as many as 300,000 in this single 30-year period.

Many nineteenth-century Irish immigrants found life difficult in ways they had sometimes experienced back in their homeland. The Irish, historically, were mistreated by English authorities, many of whom thought of them as lazy, heavy-drinking, irresponsible, and always ready for a fight. These stereotypes found a place in America, too, where many, especially those of English descent, expressed negative attitudes toward the Irish on American shores. Such terms as an "Irish personality" or "Irish character" were common stereotypes. Because many Irish immigrants who reached the United States were, indeed, of the poorer class, the prejudices seemed to ring true. During the nineteenth century and even well into the twentieth, there was a general discrimination that was applied generally to any immigrant of Irish descent. Jobs were difficult to come by, except for unskilled, menial positions.

In the 1840s and 1850s, the trickle of Irish immigrating to America became a tidal wave. In the five years between 1846 and

1851, more than one million Irish left their traditional homes, took passage on great-masted ships, and sailed to America. Irish flooded to America because of a destructive potato famine back home. Large numbers of Irish seeking better lives in North America (they immigrated not only to the United States, but also to Canada) continued to make their way across the Atlantic for the remainder of the nineteenth century. Nearly 900,000 came between 1860 and 1880, followed by another million during the next 20 years. They traveled across the cold waters of the North Atlantic under difficult conditions. Given their general poverty, the Irish could only afford to buy tickets in the ships' steerage (or poorer accommodations):

> For $50, no small sum for an impoverished immigrant, passengers were crammed into a cargo ship with as many as 900 others, allotted only as much space as their bodies took up, their possessions tightly rolled up by their sides. Worse, filth and human excrement were everywhere. And cholera and other fatal illnesses, often brought on board by diseased immigrants, stalked the ship like a stowaway.[28]

Such poor travel conditions were only part of the picture. Laws intended to improve the shipboard conditions for the Irish and others who were stuffed below decks in steerage were passed in both the United States and Great Britain, but few ships actually adhered to them. In addition, there was no privacy, including for women. The food was substandard and consisted typically of nothing more than "rough grain, served as a hardened lump."[29] Irish passengers suffered mistreatment at the hands of ship crews, who swore at them, expressed anger at them, and sometimes beat them or abused them with other forms of physical violence. If Irish passengers died during their voyage to America, their bodies were simply dumped overboard with little or no ceremony.

DISCRIMINATION AGAINST THE IRISH

Once Irish immigrants reached American ports, their difficulties were not over—they continued to experience prejudice and wholesale discrimination. The Irish remained in Eastern cities in larger percentages than other European immigrant groups, such as Scandinavians or Germans. Whereas other immigrants often fanned out across the country, seeking new lives on unsettled lands, "the Irish seldom lit out for the unpopulated frontier."[30] Generally, all that awaited them out West was another life of agriculture. Because the Irish Potato Famine of the 1840s drove many to America, these displaced Irish farmers were in no hurry to return to farming, especially potatoes. In addition, because many Irish immigrants were Catholic, they chose to remain in the Eastern cities, where Catholic churches were commonplace. The result was a high concentration of unskilled, poor, often illiterate Irish in America's Eastern urban centers, because "for the rural Irish who emigrated to America, cities offered the only way they saw to improve their social and economic positions."[31]

By 1850, the majority of the recently arrived Irish immigrants were clustered in four states: three in the East—Massachusetts, New York, and Pennsylvania—plus Illinois. About half the Irish population in the United States lived in these states, where they constituted a dramatic example of an underclass in American society. Black slaves were the abused work force in the South during these decades, whereas the Irish were abused in the North in various ways. Part of that abuse took the form of discrimination:

> Penniless and unskilled, these refugees from a land racked by starvation took whatever jobs they could find, for any wage. In the 1830s, unskilled laborers received about $1.00 per working day. A decade later, even as business boomed, wages dropped to less than 75 cents for a 10- or 12-hour working day.[32]

This 1898 Charles Joseph Staniland print depicts a wave of Irish citizens arriving in the United States. Irish immigrants arrived in record-breaking numbers in the nineteenth century and generally were treated poorly.

Even with Irish workers accepting these minimum wages, many of them found it difficult to find work at all. Prejudice caused many would-be employers advertising for workers to refuse to accept applications from the Irish. Sometimes a job listing or a "Help Wanted" sign in a storefront, shop, or other place of business put the prejudice in no uncertain terms. It was not uncommon before the Civil War for Irish workers looking for jobs to read such signs as "No Irish Need Apply." (Sometimes such advertisements for labor were not obvious in their prejudices. Some work ads specified that applicants must be practicing Protestants, a restriction that eliminated the vast majority of Irish because nearly all were Roman Catholics.)

IRISH OPPORTUNITIES DENIED

The living conditions that many of these urbanized Irish endured were appalling. Some landlords would not rent rooms to Irish workers, and others set prices beyond their means. Consequently, Irish immigrants took lodging where they could find it, usually in the most run-down areas of cities. Sometimes they crammed into basement and cellar rooms with "as many as forty immigrants . . . crowded into a single cellar space in the developing slums of Boston and New York where the most destitute lived, and where their death rates were virtually as high as they had been in Irish rural areas during the famine."[33] Such compact urban living sometimes led to violence and petty crime. Fighting by some hard-drinking, rowdy Irish led urban police to refer to the wagons they used to haul those arrested to jail as "Paddy wagons." (*Paddy* was a common slur name used to identify Irish immigrants. It was a variation of the Irish name for "Patrick," *Padraic*.) Irish city dwellers sometimes formed gangs to provide protection for themselves and to carry out criminal activity. These activities only reinforced the prejudices that many Americans had about the Irish.

These same prejudices made it difficult for nineteenth-century American Irish to achieve and to move up the socioeconomic ladder. The vast majority of Irish immigrant laborers in America did not have enough money or investment capital to start their own businesses. The result was that often Irish workers could get only manual labor–type work in the nation's developing factory system, or in mills, mines, and other industries needing difficult, unskilled labor. Even when hired on at such places, Irish workers often remained stuck in the same job for years, without advancement.

Despite hard work and dedication to a given employer, "the Irish were seldom promoted to supervisory positions because the companies went outside to hire Yankee supervisors."[34] This meant that although Irish employees worked hard at jobs that required backbreaking labor and paid low wages, they remained poor. This created a cycle of discrimination and prejudice. Because Irish families were often poverty-stricken, children of Irish workers often entered the work force at an earlier age than did those from other groups. Like their parents, they, too, rarely had other opportunities, which led them into the same kinds of destructive work patterns that their parents were bound to. This phenomenon of low wages was not unique to Irish men and boys. Irish women migrated to America in large numbers, eventually matching the number of men who immigrated. They, too, needed jobs and accepted menial work, often as domestic servants such as cooks and maids. Many of them worked for rock-bottom wages that might average 50 cents a week plus room and board.

During the decade before the Civil War, male and female Irish workers faced lives of underpaid and constant labor. In the 1850s, about one out of every five workers was unskilled in the United States, but among the general immigrant worker population, about 35 percent were unskilled. Among the Irish, it was even higher. In New York City, one out of four Irish workers could be described as follows:

> laborers, carters, porters, and waiters, with another 25 percent in domestic service and 10 percent in the garment trade operating newly invented sewing machines. This put at least 50 percent at the lowest rung of the occupational ladder. In the same decade, 55 percent of those arrested for crime in New York City were Irish-born.[35]

Even following the Civil War, the Irish in America continued to be the victims of widespread prejudice. Their poverty continued. As late as 1860, the national census counted 1.6 million Irish still living in the East, especially in the states of New Jersey, New York, Pennsylvania, and the eastern region of New England. The vast majority were poor and still unskilled. (Many of the wealthier Irish immigrants tended to move out of the cities and spread out across the country.) The attitude that Irish were shiftless and drunkards would dominate in America into the twentieth century.

DISCRIMINATION AGAINST OTHER GROUPS

Discriminatory attitudes toward and policies against immigrants in America were not limited to the Irish. Other ethnic and racial groups were sometimes equally despised. There were Americans opposed to Jews and Eastern Europeans, including Hungarians, Italians, Slavs, and others. The more immigrants of a given ethnic background who reached America, the more opposed some native-born Americans were to them. The nineteenth-century American press usually supported such prejudices and the discriminatory practices they fostered. In the mid-1870s, a Chicago newspaper described a group of Bohemian immigrants who had arrived recently in the city as "depraved beasts, harpies, decayed physically and spiritually, mentally and morally, thievish and licentious."[36] Ten years later, in response to the number of East Europeans arriving in Chicago, another city paper editorialized, "Let us whip these slavic wolves back to the European dens from which they issue, or in some way exterminate them."[37]

DISCRIMINATION AGAINST THE CHINESE

Blacks and European immigrants faced social challenges and racism in America during the nineteenth century, but they were not alone. Other ethnic minorities were also mistreated and victimized by racism and discriminatory practices by the vast, white majority. One such group was the Chinese. Although few Chinese lived in America during the first half of the 1800s, they flocked to California by the 1850s and the following decades, lured by the discoveries of gold in the remote mining camps near Sacramento. Between 1868 and 1882, about 160,000 Chinese left their traditional homes and emigrated to the United States, most electing to live along the West Coast, generally in California.

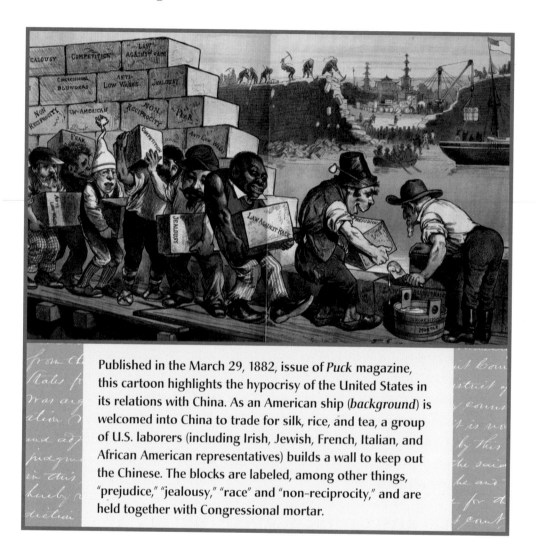

Published in the March 29, 1882, issue of *Puck* magazine, this cartoon highlights the hypocrisy of the United States in its relations with China. As an American ship (*background*) is welcomed into China to trade for silk, rice, and tea, a group of U.S. laborers (including Irish, Jewish, French, Italian, and African American representatives) builds a wall to keep out the Chinese. The blocks are labeled, among other things, "prejudice," "jealousy," "race" and "non-reciprocity," and are held together with Congressional mortar.

Many Chinese came from their homelands not necessarily to prospect for gold, but rather to serve as workers, taking jobs as day laborers and launderers, washing the clothes of the miners. So many Chinese (most were men) concentrated in the region of the gold mining camps that they became a target to the white population, who were often motivated only by racism. The Chinese were typically discriminated against. When some Chinese banded together and began working the abandoned diggings of white prospectors, the state of California, in

1850, passed the Foreign Miners' Tax. To escape such unfair and discriminatory laws, some Chinese miners moved to mining camps in other places, such as Nevada, Idaho, Colorado, and Montana. In nearly every place, new state and territorial laws were passed, allowing new forms of discrimination against the Chinese.

When Chinese workers tried their hand at other work, discrimination followed them there as well. Between 1860 and 1890, California landowners employed many Chinese field hands, who helped develop valuable farms, orchards, and vineyards from unproductive lands. Although the Chinese were recognized as hard workers, by the 1870s, many whites turned against them when a serious depression gripped the nation. Unemployed whites came to believe they had lost their jobs to industrious Chinese workers, which resulted in increased tensions and riots.

In the summer of 1871, a serious riot erupted that involved thousands of whites, who attacked the Chinese living in a "Chinatown" in Los Angeles. The riot lasted for three days, as racism drove the rioters to burn homes and Chinese-run shops. Many defenseless Chinese were robbed and beaten, and several were killed. Some Chinese men were attacked and their queues (or pigtails) cut off by white men, who then wore them as souvenirs. These sorts of attacks against the Chinese were often led by Irish men, who felt their livelihood was threatened by Chinese who worked hard for low wages. The irony is, of course, that the Irish themselves were being discriminated against similarly in other parts of the country at the same time! Even though the rampage destroyed the lives of many of the southern California town's Chinese inhabitants, law officials and local authorities did nothing, and the Chinese were helpless to respond. Even if prosecutions had taken place, a state law passed in California in 1863 forbade Chinese to testify in court against any white man.

During the 1860s, many Chinese laborers were hired to work in railroad construction. Between 1864 and 1869, a transcontinental rail line was being built that would link different areas of the country. The line was to run from Omaha, Nebraska, to Sacramento, California. With so many men working the mining camps in California, railroad workers were too few. By 1865, however, the Central Pacific Railroad was hiring Chinese laborers by the hundreds. Within just two years, 12,000 of the railroad's 13,500 workers were Chinese immigrants. Although the Chinese were hard workers who were extremely reliable and capable of working with explosives, they were typically looked down on by white workers. Even the most industrious Chinese workers were victimized by mistreatment, discrimination, and racism at the hands of whites.

RESTRICTED BY LAW

Discrimination against Chinese immigrants to America did not end during the nineteenth century. Although the Chinese tried to adapt to every slight against them, changing their lives and means of making a living many times over, laws were constantly enacted in places such as California to restrict their advancement. When Chinese workers began producing cigars that competed with American cigars, American cigar makers protested. Labor unions attempted to protect American-made cigars by trying to organize a boycott of Chinese cigars, but the average cigar buyer could not tell the difference between a Chinese-made cigar and one that was American-made. One labor leader, Samuel Gompers, head of the American Federation of Labor, one of America's most powerful labor unions, was opposed to immigrant labor, including the Chinese, taking "American" jobs. (He not only thought that these Asian immigrants were "ignorant, unskilled, and unassimilable"[38] to the American way of life, but he also thought the same of immigrants from Eastern and Southern Europe.) In Gompers' words, "Some way must be found to safeguard

America."[39] To solve the Chinese versus American cigar problem, he proposed that American-made cigars have a paper band placed around them to identify them. As the idea caught on, it appeared to work, and soon Chinese cigar makers were pushed out of business.

Other laws targeting the Chinese were passed. During the late 1800s, cities passed ordinances against the Chinese, although the laws typically did not refer to the Chinese specifically. One such law, the Cubic Air Ordinance, was passed in 1871. Under this ordinance, each adult was required to have at least 500 cubic feet of living space. Since many Chinese men shared lodgings, sometimes crowding a dozen people into a single room, the law posed a problem for them. As a result, police would sometimes raid a local "Chinatown" and round up hundreds of Chinese, taking them to jail for violating the city code. Ironically, when local jails became overcrowded with Chinese inmates, the Chinese accused city officials of breaking their own ordinances! As a result, in time, such laws were often repealed.

Other such laws, usually aimed at restricting the trade and business carried out by Chinese workers, were passed in California. In 1870, a Sidewalk Ordinance made it illegal for anyone to walk along a sidewalk carrying his goods on long poles. This was a traditional Chinese method of hauling things, so the law's only intent was to hamper the Chinese way. Another such law, the Laundry Ordinance, was passed in 1873 in several locations. This law required anyone carrying laundry on foot and not using a horse-drawn wagon or cart to purchase a high-priced license. Because the Chinese were usually the only ones who carried their laundry by hand, they were obviously the targets of the law.

By the early 1880s, discriminatory practices against the Chinese had reached a peak. Many thought the Chinese either were making too much money or were taking jobs that might otherwise go to whites. (Never mind that many Chinese did work that a lot of whites would not do.) Pushed by labor organizations and unions, the U.S. Congress passed the Chinese Exclusion Act in 1882. This piece of legislation banned the entrance of new Chinese immigrants to the country for ten years. The law exempted only a handful of Chinese teachers, students, businessmen, and tourists. West Coast states were particularly hard hit. Although 40,000 Chinese lived in California at the time the act was passed, that number would not increase for the next several years. In 1887, for example, only ten Chinese immigrants were given admittance to California.

NATIVISM: THE POLITICS OF DISCRIMINATION

Discrimination fostered against Irish and Chinese immigrants to America in the nineteenth century was not limited to those two groups. The century would be known for several movements targeting immigrants. Those who decried the increasing numbers of immigrants to the United States are often called "nativists," and their negative, perhaps even paranoid, racism is called "nativism." A significant nativist movement took place during the 1840s and 1850s. With the massive wave of immigrants from Ireland and Germany reaching America, especially after 1845, many Americans began to decry this increased level of immigration with antiforeign and anti-Catholic reactions. Between 1846 and 1855, 3 million foreigners reached American shores, many crowding into the cities of the East and Midwest. The immediate result was that such cities as Chicago, Milwaukee, New York, and St. Louis were home to more foreign-born immigrants than native-born citizens.

Nativists, those opposed to open immigration, campaigned against these new arrivals, drumming up the emotionally based fears of Protestants and working-class people, who worried that immigrants

In a follow-up move to hamper Chinese living in America, in 1888, Congress passed the Scott Act. The act forbade Chinese who left the United States to re-enter the country. Because the vast majority of Chinese living in the United States were male, many Chinese men returned to their homeland to find wives and bring them to America. The Scott Act would no longer allow them to do so. (There were other laws on the books, as well, that did not allow Chinese men to marry anyone but Chinese women, so the law was especially restrictive.) When the Exclusion Act of 1882 had run through its ten-year

would take their jobs by accepting lower wages. One anti-Catholic organization, "The Order of the Star Spangled Banner," was made up of these native-born Protestant workers. This group soon developed into a full-blown political party, the Know-Nothing, or American, Party. (The "Know-Nothing" name came about because the group's members agreed not to talk about the inner workings of their party; they would answer questions with "I know nothing.")

By 1855, the Know-Nothings were politically consolidating their power. That year, they gained control of several New England state legislatures and were the dominant opposition party to the Democrats in New York, Pennsylvania, Virginia, Tennessee, Georgia, Alabama, Mississippi, Maryland, and Louisiana. Between 1853 and 1855, the nativist Know-Nothings became the second largest political party in America—larger than the declining Whig Party. Although the party would not last long (it was nearly dead by 1856), it served as a reminder of the depth of the animosity many Americans leveraged toward ethnic immigrant groups.

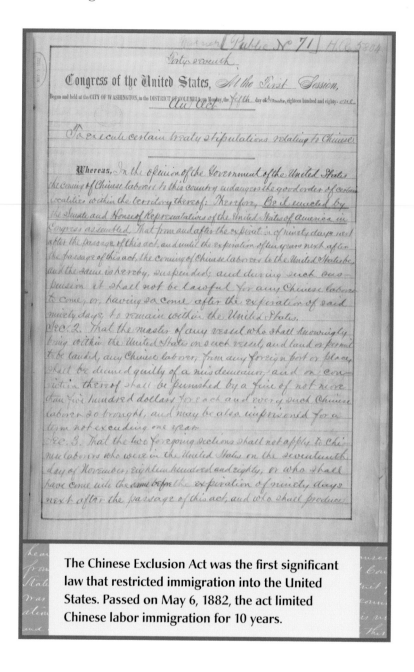

The Chinese Exclusion Act was the first significant law that restricted immigration into the United States. Passed on May 6, 1882, the act limited Chinese labor immigration for 10 years.

cycle of restricting Chinese immigration, the restrictions were extended for another decade through the Geary Act of 1892. Unlike the original Chinese Exclusion Act, the Geary Act also "required Chinese who wished to remain in America to apply for a certificate of eligibility and to carry identification, exposing them to daily harassment by officials."[40] Such discrimination against the Chinese in America would continue well into the twentieth century.

3

Separate but Equal

For all the prejudices and discriminations directed against some European and Asian immigrants, racist attitudes toward and discrimination against American blacks was constant and extreme. Even following the American Civil War (1861–1865), which helped bring an end to black slavery in America, blacks continued to face prejudice and discrimination. Attempts were made by the federal government, however, to protect blacks and their newly won freedom.

THREE AMENDMENTS FOR FREEDOM
The post–Civil War Congress approved three amendments to the U.S. Constitution, all of which sought to dramatically

change the status of blacks in America. The Thirteenth Amendment was ratified in 1865. This brought slavery to an end. The following year, Congress passed the Fourteenth Amendment, which guaranteed blacks rights equal to whites as citizens of the United States. The amendment was ratified by the states by July 1868. Although the amendment was immediately aimed at the nation's blacks, it would apply to all Americans, regardless of race. As the amendment was worded:

> All persons born or naturalized in the United States . . . are citizens of the United States. . . . No State shall make or enforce any law which shall abridge the privileges or immunities of citizens of the United States; nor shall any State deprive any person of life, liberty, or property, without due process of law; nor deny to any person within its jurisdiction the equal protection of the laws.[41]

(When Allan Bakke decided to take his case to court, his attorney would claim that his equal rights had been violated—rights guaranteed to him under the Fourteenth Amendment.) With this amendment, blacks began gaining new freedoms and privileges. They could serve on juries and provide testimony in court. They could also attend schools, even integrated ones, and receive an education, a first for the vast majority of America's blacks. Then, in 1869, Congress passed a third amendment, the Fifteenth, this one intended to guarantee blacks the right to vote. (The amendment was ratified the following year.) Given these important protective laws, as well as others, blacks were able to exert their political powers as never before. Blacks voted and even elected their fellow black leaders to public office.

All was not well between the races in America, however. During the decades following the war and Emancipation, blacks struggled against a sweeping tide of white-directed discrimination aimed at every aspect of their lives. Since many whites— both Northern and Southern—continued to consider blacks as

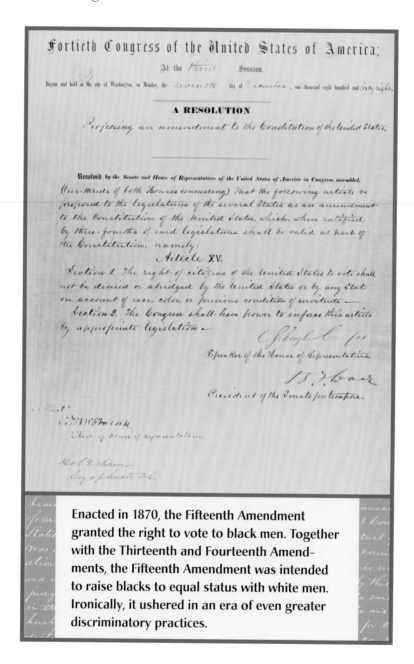

Enacted in 1870, the Fifteenth Amendment granted the right to vote to black men. Together with the Thirteenth and Fourteenth Amendments, the Fifteenth Amendment was intended to raise blacks to equal status with white men. Ironically, it ushered in an era of even greater discriminatory practices.

inferiors, they thought blacks should play a lesser role in American society.

Consequently, some positive steps were turned around. Ten years after the Civil War, Congress passed the Civil Rights Act of

1875. It was intended to ban discrimination. The act stated that "All persons . . . shall be entitled to the full and equal enjoyment of the accommodations, advantages, facilities, and privileges of inns, public conveyances on land or water, theaters, and other places of public amusement."[42] The law was yet another well-intended act of Congress designed to provide equal rights to blacks. In the years that followed, though, between 1875 and 1900, blacks, especially those in the South, saw their freedoms slipping away. Segregation became the law of the land.

Thousands of "Jim Crow" laws were passed by white-controlled Southern legislatures during those years, forcing blacks out of the mainstream of American cultural, social, and economic life. Blacks were denied significant jobs, and they were discriminated against in public places. By 1883, the U.S. Supreme Court had declared the Civil Rights Act of 1875 unconstitutional through the court's decision in the Civil Rights Cases of 1883. This decision allowed hotels, railroads, and "places of public amusement" to discriminate without breaking the law. (Following that decision, the U.S. government largely withdrew from the enforcement of civil rights until after World War II) Blacks were denied access to first-class railroad cars and other means of public transportation. They were treated across the South as second-class citizens.

DISCRIMINATION BY LAW

One of the most significant ways blacks were discriminated against during these final decades of the nineteenth century, as well as during the first 50 years of the twentieth century, was in education. Many states operated separate schools for their black students, schools that were commonly inferior to the schools provided for white children. When a Supreme Court case, *Plessy v. Ferguson*, established the theory of "separate but equal" as the law of the land in 1896, segregation and discrimination would mark the lives of nearly every black person in the South. Everything from lunch counters to libraries, parks to public accommodations, and drinking fountains to toilets were separated by law, always under the false expectation of "separate but equal." Schools were no exception.

During the first half of the twentieth century, however, organizations with both black and white membership began to campaign against discrimination in America's schools— specifically, against segregation. "Separate but equal" had only resulted in schools becoming more "separate"; they were almost never equal, with black schools almost always offering fewer opportunities. Such black schools were underfunded, lacked adequate facilities and equipment, had low-paid teachers, and sometimes had no textbooks. Such groups typically filed lawsuits against various schools, hoping the courts would decide in their favor and order changes that would bring improvements to black schools. In time, these same organizations were fighting not for "equal" and still separate schools, but instead were taking schools to court to bring about integration.

Once such organization was the National Association for the Advancement of Colored People (NAACP), which was established in 1910 in New York City. This organization was destined to become the most important American civil rights organization of the twentieth century. Its legal wing, later called the Legal Defense Fund, would lead the vanguard in taking cases to court, in an effort to bring about desegregation and eliminate discrimination in schools. The organization made little progress for several years, failing to win key court battles over segregated schools. Victories did come eventually, however.

Under the leadership of Charles Houston, dean of the law school at Howard University (a historically black school), the NAACP was able to win key education cases. One of its earliest was a 1936 decision, *Pearson v. Murray*, which opened up the University of Maryland's law school to blacks. In this case, the Maryland Court of Appeals agreed that Donald Murray, a black applicant, had been denied "admission [to the University of Maryland] on the sole ground of his color."[43] Working

Charles Houston (standing, right) won many landmark discrimination cases as special counsel to the NAACP, including *Pearson v. Murray* and *Missouri ex rel. Gaines v. Canada*. Those victories and others that were won after Houston's death laid the groundwork for Allan Bakke's case.

alongside Houston on the Murray case was a young black attorney who had graduated from Howard Law School three years earlier. He would one day serve on the U.S. Supreme Court and was a justice when Bakke filed his lawsuit against the University of California, Davis medical school—Thurgood Marshall.

Throughout the late 1930s, the NAACP took other race discrimination cases, each connected to education, to court. In 1938, the civil rights organization and Charles Houston won another case, *State of Missouri ex rel. Gaines v. Canada*. This case centered on a black student, Lloyd Gaines, who, after graduating from Lincoln University, a black school in Jefferson City, Missouri, applied to the University of Missouri Law School, but was denied entrance because of his race. The Supreme Court decided in favor of Gaines. It was determined that the laws of Missouri had denied Gaines his guarantee of equal rights under the Fourteenth Amendment. The *Murray* decision had impacted the state of Maryland, but the *Gaines* case would have a national impact. The following year, Charles Houston decided to leave the NAACP's legal wing and take up private practice with his father. With his departure in the spring of 1939, Thurgood Marshall stepped into his shoes.

Over the next ten years, Marshall, as the lead attorney for its Legal Defense Fund, led the offensive on behalf of the NAACP. He took on a Maryland county school board for paying black teachers less than white teachers and won. He won a similar case in Virginia in 1940. Marshall and the NAACP took other civil rights cases, outside the field of education. They won a 1941 case, *Mitchell v. United States,* which focused on an Arkansas law requiring blacks to ride in inferior railroad cars. He succeeded in winning a 1944 case against a Texas law that denied blacks the right to vote in primary elections. Another case in Maryland centered on a black woman who refused to sit on the back seat of a bus in Baltimore. Again, Marshall won his case.

Other education cases followed, both victories for Thurgood Marshall: *Sweatt v. Painter* resulted in the entrance of a black man to the University of Texas Law School, whereas *McLaurin v. Oklahoma State Regents for Higher Education* gave another black man, George McLaurin, the opportunity to enroll into a doctoral education program at the University of Oklahoma. Both cases were decided by the U.S. Supreme Court on the same day, in April 1950. With these victories, by 1950, the legacy of "separate but equal," and the continuing impact (more than a half century's worth) of *Plessy v. Ferguson* seemed closer to an end.

Over the next four years, Marshall and his colleagues at the NAACP would line up a group of cases in an attempt to finally destroy "separate but equal." Collectively known as *Brown v.*

Linda (left) and Terry Lynn Brown pose outside their segregated elementary school in Topeka, Kansas, in March 1953. The Brown family's landmark Supreme Court case, *Brown v. Board of Education* resulted in an integrated public school system.

Board of Education of Topeka, the case drove the final nail in *Plessy v. Ferguson's* coffin. The cases that composed the Brown case before the U.S. Supreme Court were concerned with discrimination in public schools, including elementary and high schools. The case gave the Supreme Court the opportunity to rule "in the NAACP's favor on the equality issue."[44] The Supreme Court would have to deal with the important question of whether segregation could be allowed, given the equal protection clause of the Fourteenth Amendment.

When the Supreme Court finally rendered its decision on this important set of cases on May 17, 1954, it was a bombshell against discrimination in education. The court decided to overturn *Plessy v. Ferguson*. No longer would the concept of "separate but equal" continue as the law of the land. In making its unanimous decision, the court agreed with Marshall and his fellow attorneys, who had argued that the use of race to determine someone's educational status was a violation of the Fourteenth Amendment. The *Brown* decision would serve as the greatest and most important civil rights case of the twentieth century. Within a generation, however, another important race and education case was going to make its mark, as well. The white aerospace engineer from California, Allan Bakke, would prove to be the catalyst for this important U.S. Supreme Court decision.

Bakke Applies to Medical School

4

B efore Allan Bakke ever considered filing a discrimination lawsuit in federal court, it would have been inconceivable that he would find himself needing to take such a significant step. He did not, after all, fit the profile of someone who was part of a typically downtrodden or oppressed group, one that had been discriminated against historically. He was not a member of a minority group. In appearance, he looked the same as the vast majority of other Americans. Growing up, he had never, to his knowledge, been denied anything that other American citizens generally had available to them. He was, as described by the *New York Times* during his famous court battle, a tall, "fair-skinned, blond-haired, daily jogger, . . .

a husky baldish father of two [who has] a personal obsession to become a physician."[45]

THE SON OF A POSTAL WORKER

In many ways, Allan Bakke's background reflected that of many middle-class Americans. He had never been wealthy or enjoyed the advantages of privilege. He was a man raised on Midwestern values. Born in February 1940 in Minneapolis, Minnesota, Bakke was the son of a postal worker and a school teacher. His family came from Norwegian stock. During his early years, the Bakkes moved from the frigid environments of the north central states to sunny Florida. Allan's heart remained in the North, however, and when it came time for college, he returned to Minneapolis to attend the University of Minnesota. There, he studied and majored in mechanical engineering and graduated in 1962 with a grade point average just under an A—3.51. While studying engineering, he had been elected to the national mechanical engineering honor society. Because his family did not have enough money to support him during his college years, Bakke helped pay for his schooling by joining the campus unit of the naval ROTC (Reserve Officers' Training Corps).

Bakke graduated from the university with a degree in high demand. The American space program was just hitting its stride, having launched its first human into space in the spring of 1961. As an engineer, Bakke was the kind of university graduate that NASA was looking for, but he needed more study. Bakke was accepted to graduate school and continued his studies for a year. Then, his military obligations through the ROTC program took him away from his academic work. He had to honor his military agreement and serve in the armed services. He elected to serve as an officer in the U.S. Marine Corps and served a four-year commitment, from 1963 until 1967. During those years, he served in the field as a Marine captain, on a combat tour in Vietnam.

Bakke completed his military duties in 1967, then returned to civilian life and his academic work. He attended Stanford University, where he began work on a master's degree in engineering. He was quickly approached by NASA and began working at the Ames Research Center, south of San Francisco. He and his family (by this time he had married and had three children) soon settled down to life in California, where Bakke went to work as an aerospace engineer. He continued taking classes at Stanford and completed his Master of Arts degree in 1970. Bakke proved an asset to the research work being done at the Ames facility. His direct supervisor, David Engelbert, gave Bakke high marks, saying "I don't know anyone brighter or more capable."[46]

Allan Bakke, photographed here in October 1977, was not willing to compromise his dream of becoming a doctor.

Although Allan Bakke appeared to have found his niche, his professional place in the world, and all seemed well, he was not satisfied. Through his studies and regular contact with medical personnel assigned to the Ames facility, Bakke developed a strong desire to become a doctor. Not content to merely dream of being a medical doctor, Bakke began taking steps that pointed him in that direction. Writing years later, the frustrated aerospace engineer explained: "I undertook a near full-time course load of medical prerequisites—biology and chemistry. To make up class and commuting hours, I worked early mornings and also evenings at my job."[47] In 1971, Bakke began taking night classes at San Jose State University, as well as at Stanford. He managed to knock out all the prerequisites needed for him to apply and be accepted to medical school. He even volunteered to work during his off hours at an emergency room at El Camino Hospital in Mountain View, California. While there, he asked for the "tough assignments, often working late with battered victims of car accidents or fights."[48] This well-paid, professional engineer wanted to become something else—something, he believed, he was supposed to do as his life's work. Turning his dream of attending medical school into reality, however, would prove to be an uphill climb.

SEEKING A SCHOOL

In 1973, driven by his desire to become a doctor, Bakke made application to at least a dozen medical schools across the country. Some were in California, but some were far from his home— as far away as Maine. In every case, he was turned down. As discussed earlier, Allan Bakke's problem in being accepted to medical school had little or nothing to do with his grades or his general academic record or abilities. He had taken the requisite entrance tests for medical school and had performed well. His scientific knowledge placed him in the top 3 percent of those taking such tests. He scored in the high 90s on verbal ability and had a 94th percentile score in mathematics. His grade point average was adequate. There was nothing that should have disqualified him from being accepted into medical school, with one exception, one he thought might prove to be a problem from the day he filled out his first application in 1973—his age.

That year, Bakke turned 33 years old, nearly 10 years older than the average age of medical students in America. It was something Bakke could not change or address, other than to admit it and hope it did not matter. He had explored and researched the topic of his age and its relevance for medical school acceptance nearly from the first time he began thinking about becoming a doctor. In 1971, before making a single application to any such schools, he sent letters of inquiry to a dozen medical schools, asking them to specify their policy concerning age. Some schools, including the University of California, Davis, responded with explanations. They explained that "when an applicant is over 30, his age is a serious factor." The committee went on to explain that one of the major reasons for such a position was that "an applicant can be expected on an actuarial basis to practice medicine for about ten years less than the applicant of average age."[49]

The explanation was not satisfactory to Bakke. It was not as though he had been directionless in his life through his 20s and had only decided in his early 30s that it was time to make something of himself. He had already gone to undergraduate and graduate school, had received diplomas from both, and had spent six years as a professional, as something akin to the proverbial "rocket scientist." He also knew that he had "lost" four years of his earlier life by serving in the military and in Vietnam. He could not think of any of those years as having been wasted. He had developed already as an academic, a professional, and a scientist. He was now asking to take all of these previous successes in life to the next level. In his applications to the medical school at Davis, Bakke mentioned his military service, "Four years was a high price to pay for my undergraduate education and I would hope the admissions committee will not hold those years of service to America against me."[50]

He stated the obvious in his applications for medical school—that he was older than the average applicant—so that school officials would understand that he knew his age might be used as criteria for nonacceptance. In his application to the medical school at the University of California, Davis, Bakke put his cards on the table:

> I have an excellent job in engineering and am well-paid. I don't wish to change careers for financial gain, but because I truly believe my contribution to society can be much greater as a physician-engineer than in my present field. . . . More than anything else in the world, I want to study medicine."[51]

Bakke's life, as he laid it out in his application, was exactly as he described it. Not lavishly wealthy by any means, still, he was living the good life in northern California, together with his family, in an affluent neighborhood of Los Altos. They shared a comfortable home and enjoyed a world that could be afforded by an aerospace engineer. All of this simply did not matter, though, in Bakke's increasing desire to become a medical doctor.

That Bakke put his age forward on his applications as an issue was an important recognition on his part. Indeed, some of the schools he applied to did consider his age to be problematic. Northwestern University responded, informing Bakke that his age was "above their stated limit."[52] Officials at the University of California, San Francisco, were just as blunt, telling the engineer that his age was certainly a "negative factor."[53] Davis, as has already been stated, made the same point, even though the school had no clearly stated, definitive, official age restriction.

SEPARATING THE APPLICANTS

For Bakke, the University of California, Davis, was one of his first choices for medical school. It would be one of the most convenient places for him to attend classes, given its proximity to his

The admissions practices of the University of California, Davis, medical school raised the ire of the already-frustrated Allen Bakke.

home. Yet Davis became one of Bakke's greatest frustrations. When he made his first application to Davis, he was among 2,464 applicants vying for 100 slots. These medical students would start the program in the fall of 1973. The competition would be stiff, if indicated only by the sheer numbers of interested applicants.

As Davis received the applications for medical school, administrators separated them into three groups. Those applying who considered themselves "economically and educationally disadvantaged" were given the option of checking a special box on their application.[54] Applications with the box checked "Yes" were placed in their own group. Those applications with the box checked "No" were placed in a second stack. Then, the "No" applications were examined for grade point averages. All the "No" applications with a GPA of less than 2.5 (on a 4.0 scale) were systematically denied. Those applicants were informed that their application had been turned down on the basis of grades. Those "No" applications with a grade point higher than 2.5 were sent to the medical school's regular admissions committee. At this point, two groups—the admissions committee and an admissions subgroup called the "Task Force"—began filtering through the remaining two stacks of applications.

When Bakke began to prepare to apply to Davis in 1972, he was facing serious problems at home. His mother-in-law

 A POLICY OF PREFERENCES

At the time that the University of California, Davis, medical school established its Task Force to review the applications of minority candidates, only about 800 minority students were attending medical schools in the United States. Four out of five were attending two schools that were traditionally institutions for black students: Howard University's medical school, located in the nation's capital, and Meharry Medical School in Nashville, Tennessee. (Small numbers of minority students were also attending law schools in America at that time.) With the rise of the civil rights movement through the 1960s, however, blacks and other minorities were becoming intent on attending institutions of higher learning, including medical schools. With this great increase in minority applications, but with a limited number of places available for candidates to gain admittance, during the late 1960s, schools across America began to establish admissions programs based on preferential treatment for applications submitted by minorities. These "set aside" programs opened up seats for minority students, which led to an increase in the number of white applicants who were rejected for admittance to medical schools.

In 1966, the medical school at Davis opened its doors for the first time, with an entering class of 48. At that time, Davis was one of was struggling with lung cancer, and Bakke and his wife were constantly seeing to her needs. With this distraction, Bakke did not complete his application to Davis until January 9, 1973. At the time, it did not appear that the delay would prove to be a problem for the eager aerospace engineer. His grades were high and his tests scores enviable, and he already had professional experience in at least one field of the sciences. As proof, he received a letter inviting him to Davis for an interview, which was standard procedure. In fact, Bakke was "among the one out of

five medical schools within the University of California system. The others were located at Los Angeles, San Diego, San Francisco, and Irvine. Each medical school in the system created its own admissions system; policies differed in detail from one university site to the next.

During its first four years, the Davis-based medical school included no preferential or "set aside" program in its admissions policy. Through those early years, only 3 out of every 100 applications the medical school received were from minorities. Then, in 1970, the school policy changed. Administrators at Davis decided to establish a preferential or "affirmative action" admissions program. The purpose of the change in policy was to make Davis more attractive and accessible to minority students. One of the objectives of the program was to "enhance diversity in the student body and the profession, eliminate historic barriers for medical careers for disadvantaged racial and ethnic minority groups, and increase aspiration for such careers on the part of members of those groups."[*]

*Quoted in Howard Ball, *The Bakke Case: Race, Education, and Affirmative Action.* Lawrence, University Press of Kansas, 2000, p. 49.

six invited to Davis for an interview."[55] It was at this point that Bakke's "late" application may have begun to work against him. Generally, medical schools choose the candidates they are interested in over a stretch of time, not all at once. Bakke's delayed application meant that he was not slated to appear before the applications committee until March 21, 1973. By that date, the university had interviewed several applicants and had actually already mailed out acceptance letters to 123 candidates, 23 more than the number of openings for the fall class! (It was common for medical schools to accept more students than openings, since candidates are usually being considered by several universities at the same time and candidates routinely turn down one medical school's offer for another's.) By the time Bakke had his interview with Davis admissions officials, the medical school only intended to send out 37 more letters of acceptance. The odds for Bakke's acceptance were shrinking, in part because of his delayed application.[56]

Other things seemed to be falling into place for Allan Bakke. He interviewed with Dr. Theodore West, one of the faculty members at the Davis medical school, and the interview seemed to go well. West responded to the candidate's demeanor and appearance, stating that Bakke was a pleasant and mature young man. The doctor was impressed by Bakke's volunteer experiences in hospital emergency medicine and was equally pleased with the candidate's intent to mix his engineering expertise with his interest in medicine. The Davis faculty member, however, noted that Bakke, during the interview did have one subject he seemed to struggle with:

> He seems completely unprepossessing. He was not dynamic or aggressive and articulated well in all areas except his response to my request that he express for me some of his reasons for changing from engineering to medicine. During that phase his conversation was more halting, more introspective and I sensed an air of frustration and emotion

which I attribute to his concern about the impact of age and the fact that this is probably about the last chance for him to apply.[57]

West went on to state that Bakke was "a well-qualified candidate for admission whose main handicap is the unavoidable fact that he is now 33 years of age."[58] West was not the only one to interview Bakke. Another school official met with him, and emerged from his interview to describe him as "a very desirable applicant to this medical school and I shall so recommend him."[59] Bakke's application continued through the channels at Davis. His file was handed to five other admissions committee members, who were to evaluate Bakke by his test scores, GPA, and submitted recommendations, and by Dr. West's comments.

Even as Bakke's application moved along through the Davis process, the admissions Task Force was consulting their stack of applications. This admissions subgroup was made up largely of minority faculty members, as well as students. The Task Force had only been established in 1969, "to help bring greater diversity into the medical school."[60]

As a result, Davis officials set aside 16 percent—8 out of 50 potential medical students—of the available seats for the medical school class beginning that fall for minorities who considered themselves "disadvantaged." (This was, of course, the reason for Line 22 on the application form, the line that asked applicants if they considered themselves "economically and educationally disadvantaged." In fact, from 1970 through 1974, the medical school at Davis "admitted almost no African-American or Hispanic-American applicants who were not 'disadvantaged.'"[61]) At the same time, the school did not enroll even one white candidate who considered himself "disadvantaged."

5

The Task Force

Throughout the early 1970s, the "set-aside" percentage at Davis medical school remained at 16 percent. In 1971, when the school increased its class number from around 50 to 100, the number of "set asides" increased from 8 to 16. The dual track between the regular admission committee and the Task Force remained in play. The regular admissions group included a dozen faculty members and three students, who judged the applications of nonminorities and those minorities who did not consider themselves disadvantaged. Meanwhile, the Task Force handled the applications of those minority applicants who did consider themselves disadvantaged. At the time Bakke finally filed a suit against this kind of admissions policy, the Task Force had selected 132 minority candidates for the medical school, including 46 blacks, 33 Asians, one Native American, and one candidate of Asian-Hispanic heritage.

THE PROGRAM'S DETAILS

By the Davis policy, only those applicants whose GPA was higher than 2.5 were even considered. Of those, two of every five were asked to the Davis campus for an interview with school officials. During these interviews, officials asked questions related to the applicant's "personality, motivation, and other nonstatistical characteristics."[62]

After each interview, the interviewer reviewed the applicant's complete file and gave the applicant a "grade" on a 1 to 100 scale. Then, four additional committee members (the number was upped to five in 1974) reviewed the file, with each using the same 1 to 100 point scale. The five reviewers' scores were then combined and an average figured. This number became each applicant's "benchmark score." When Bakke applied to the Davis medical school in the spring of 1973, the maximum "benchmark score" possible was 500; that number was increased to 600 by the following year. It was this number, the "benchmark score," that proved problematic for Bakke:

> Bakke's main problem was that he applied late in 1973, and the benchmark scores, the rating of applicants by the admissions committee, had moved upward as places became scarce to a minimum of 470 out of 500 for admission. After Bakke's application made the rounds of the committee, he had a score of 468. There were at least 19 other applicants who scored 468 and 15 with scores of 469. Bakke's last hope would have been the alternate or waiting list, but while some applicants with scores of 468 went on the list, Bakke was not among them. The reason he might have been excluded from the waiting list was not

disclosed anywhere on [his file] and would not be revealed until much later.[63]

As for applicants who wished to be considered "disadvantaged" either economically or educationally (an applicant could claim both), their applications were handled by the Task Force. When Bakke first applied to Davis medical school, the general application asked would-be students if they wanted to be considered a member of a minority. If they indicated they did want to be considered as such, their application was routed to the Task Force. The membership of the Task Force at the time Bakke first applied to Davis included 5 white and 2 Asian faculty members, as well as 11 medical students who were minorities. The Task Force faced the sometimes difficult work

Riding the coattails of Bakke's pending case, another UC Davis medical school reject, Rita Greenwald Clancy, was admitted to the school by a federal court order.

of determining whether a student who claimed to be disadvantaged by economics or education actually was so. The committee considered common questions; these concerned whether the applicant held a job as an undergraduate, whether the applicant had interrupted his or her undergraduate work by dropping out of school and working, whether the applicant had participated in an equal educational opportunity program as an undergraduate, and how the applicant's parents were employed. If the Task Force did not determine that the applicant in question was really "disadvantaged," then the applicant's file was kicked over to the regular committee to face the normal criteria.

A REJECTION FROM DAVIS

The process of weeding out an appropriate number of applicants for the medical school's 1973 fall term was completed through the spring of that year. Bakke had to wait five months until he received a letter from Storandt, one of the assistant deans at the Davis medical school. The letter was a rejection. Storandt had worded it carefully and with respect, but the message was still the same:

> Your first letter involves us both in a situation as painful for us as for you. You did indeed fare well with our admissions committee and were rated in . . . the top 10 percent of our 2,500 applicants in the 1972–1973 season. . . .We can admit but 100 students, however, and thus are faced with the distressing task of turning aside the applications of some remarkably able and well-qualified individuals, including this year, yourself.[64]

As Storandt continued his letter, he mentioned Bakke's concern about his age. The assistant dean assured the aerospace engineer that "older applicants have successfully entered and worked in our curriculum and that your very considerable talents can and will override any questions of age in our final determinations."[65]

Then, as Storandt's letter continued, he suggested that Bakke not give up on Davis and that he should make application again under the school's Early Decision Plan for the next year's class, which would get him into the process for a second time and would move his next interview and evaluation up to October 1, less than three months away. Storandt could have easily let his letter end there, by giving Bakke advice on how he might approach the medical school with a second application, wish him good luck, and leave things at that. Storandt continued his letter, however. He suggested that Bakke might consider pursuing "research into admissions policies based on quota-oriented minority recruiting."[66] To give Bakke further information and direction, Storandt included a page that laid out Davis's minority admissions program and the role of the college's Task Force.

If Bakke was not understanding Storandt's allusions, the assistant dean spelled it out for him as clearly as possible, "I don't know whether you would consider our procedure to have the overtones of a quota or not, certainly its design has been to avoid such designation, but the fact remains that most applicants to such a program are members of ethnic minority groups."[67] Without directly suggesting that Bakke might consider a lawsuit against the application policy used by the Davis medical school, Storandt also included information on a case headed to the U.S. Supreme Court—*DeFunis v. Odegaard*—that challenged admissions programs based on race and even "suggested two authorities on the legal aspects of minority admissions [Bakke] might consult."[68] Despite all these prompts toward taking legal action against Davis, however, Storandt ended his letter with a strong suggestion that Bakke apply again and "make a second shot at Davis."[69]

Although Storandt would later deny that he prompted Bakke to file a lawsuit against Davis, there arguably could be no other reason for him to have included such information in his letter of denial to Bakke. He admitted later that, at that point in his working for Davis, he felt that the "set-aside" program at the medical school and the work of the Task Force "was unfairly excluding whites."[70] Perhaps he had made a mistake by putting the information about the college's quota system, the reference to the *DeFunis* case, and other matters that might lead to a lawsuit in his official correspondence with Bakke. Because he would meet unofficially with Bakke a month and a half after sending the letter, he could have given him the information at that time and spared himself some difficulties when Bakke did file his lawsuit. As Storandt would describe his actions later: "I overstepped my bound of propriety and authority."[71]

A NEW PLAN

Later that summer, after Bakke and Storandt had their face-to-face discussion after hours at the admissions building, Bakke began to formulate his next strategy regarding his future medical school applications. It would be more complicated than simply applying to Davis, as he already had earlier in 1973. In fact, Bakke began to shape two plans in his head. Under his first plan, he would apply to Davis under the school's Early Decision Plan, just as Storandt had suggested. Even as he would apply, however, he would sue Stanford University and the University of California, San Francisco. He would sue even if Davis allowed him to enter its medical school. Bakke was intent on suing Stanford, because he considered his chances of winning better, since Stanford officials had "stated categorically that it had set aside twelve places in its entering class for racial minorities."[72]

Bakke's second plan was only a variation on this same theme: apply and sue. This plan called for Bakke to still apply to Davis while at the same time threatening Stanford with a lawsuit in an attempt to push Stanford to admit him "as an alternative to a legal challenge of their admitted racial quota."[73] If Stanford folded and admitted him, he would then sue Davis and San Francisco. If Davis also allowed him entrance, he would still attend Stanford and only sue San Francisco.

Stanford University was one of the institutions Allan Bakke planned on suing for discrimination.

Even as Bakke formulated these two strategies, he sent a letter to Storandt thanking him for his candor during their meeting just four days earlier. In the letter he also laid out his two plans to Storandt, asking the assistant dean to help by giving him more information about Davis. When Storandt read the letter, he immediately knew he had put himself in an awkward position by providing information to Bakke. The worried assistant dean went to his superior, Dean C. John Tupper, and told him about his clandestine meeting with Bakke and the letters the two men had written to one another. Dean Tupper did not appear concerned about the situation, despite Storandt informing him that Bakke seemed intent on filing a lawsuit. Tupper took no steps in response to the matter.

Storandt might have been able to wash his hands of responsibility in the unfolding matter by ending any further contact with Bakke, but he did not. Instead, he wrote Bakke another letter, this one on August 15. In this letter, Storandt seemed as supportive as ever: "It seems to me that you have carefully arranged your thinking about this matter and that the eventual result of your next actions will be of significance to many present and future medical school applicants."[74] Storandt not only seems to have given support to Bakke, he even offered opinions on Bakke's two plans of action. The assistant dean preferred Bakke's second plan, the one calling for Bakke to apply to Stanford, Davis, and San Francisco and sue the school(s) that did not accept him. Storandt even told Bakke that the Stanford program was probably the most vulnerable to a lawsuit having to do with discrimination. He told Bakke about the performances of Davis's minority students generally, how about half of the third-year minority students failed their National Board exams on their first attempt. All this was invaluable information to Bakke. It is difficult to imagine a greater mentor and ally for Allan Bakke than Peter Storandt.

A CHANGE OF FORM

According to Bakke's plan, he did apply a second time for acceptance to Davis medical school. Only this time, Bakke was a known name and university officials had gotten wind that he might be considering suing the university based on its preferential admissions policy. When Bakke applied this second time, there was another difference. There was a new general application form.

It still asked if the applicant wanted to declare himself or herself as an "economically and/or educationally disadvantaged" candidate. Those who indicated they did, however, also checked a box identifying themselves as one of four ethnic minority groups—"Black, Chicano, Asian, and American Indian." There was a "white" or "Caucasian" box to select from, as well. (The difference on this application was that the applicant was asked to specifically identify his or her ethnic background.)

On the earlier form, race was not mentioned specifically, although most of those who applied as "disadvantaged" were one of the four minorities. Some whites had also checked the "disadvantaged" box between 1970 and 1974, though. In fact, 73 white applicants in 1973 alone had identified themselves as disadvantaged, either economically or educationally. The Task Force had not reviewed any of their applications, however. In 1974, the number of "disadvantaged" whites applying was 172. None of them were reviewed by the Task Force. Whites had learned how to play the game of preferential treatment on the Davis application forms, but the Task Force had not been willing to play.

There was another change in the process of applying to Davis for the fall class of 1974. The Davis medical school had, since the previous year, joined a national, centralized organization, the American Medical College Application System (AMCAS). This allowed would-be medical school students to fill out a single application that was then sent to all the medical schools the applicant wanted to consider him or her for acceptance. The result was a significant increase in the number of applicants to Davis, as well as to other medical schools. The previous year, Bakke had competed with nearly 2,500 applicants. For the fall 1974 term, he was up against 3,737!

On his second application, Bakke checked the box identifying him as "White/Caucasian," and he checked "No" on the box asking if he was "disadvantaged," just as he had done on his first application. As he had earlier, he mentioned his age on the application and his general concern about how it might impact his odds of being accepted into medical school. He did note his overall good health, noting that he believed he would be able to practice medicine just as long as a younger candidate might. Again, as on the earlier application, he explained why he was coming to medicine so late and emphasized the importance that becoming a doctor had for him: "More than anything else in the world, *I want to study medicine.*"[75]

There was another twist to the second application process. One of Bakke's interviews would be with a medical student. Bakke was assigned to meet with Frank Gioia, a student in his second year of medical school. When Gioia and Bakke met, the interview went well. Gioia, who was younger than Bakke, found the aerospace engineer to be "friendly, well-tempered, conscientious, and delightful to speak with."[76] The only awkward moment took place when the two discussed minority admissions. Bakke made it clear that he thought medical students should be selected based on their qualifications, not their minority status. The position was not to Gioia's liking, but the medical student gave Bakke a "sound recommendation."[77]

Bakke's other interview, this time with a faculty member named Dr. George Lowrey, did not go well. He found Bakke's position on minority students being accepted under a separate program as "unsympathetic."[78] The doctor wrote on his evaluation that Bakke was "a rather rigidly oriented young man who has the tendency to arrive at conclusions based more upon his personal impressions than upon thoughtful processes." He gave Bakke an "acceptable" but not "outstanding" rating as a candidate to the Davis medical school.[79]

As for the remainder of the selection process concerning Bakke's second application to Davis, the facts remain unclear. During the ensuing court case, no testimony ever fully explained the "relationship between grades, test scores, and interviews with the benchmark ratings," leaving the court feeling that the "rating was quite arbitrary."[80] The number of people assessing applications for the class to begin in the fall of 1974 was upped from five to six, but each scored Bakke without seeing the evaluations of any of the others.

Here, the story returns to the pertinent numbers. Of the six who evaluated Bakke, four scores were in the 90s: a 92 (Storandt), two 94s (including Gioia), and a 96. One gave him an 87, and Dr. Lowrey posted Bakke's lowest score, an 86. This made Bakke's benchmark score 549. The result was his rejection under the Early Decision Plan in the fall of 1973, as well as another rejection in the spring of 1974. When comparing Bakke's scores to other applicants, interesting number comparisons can be made. A dozen applicants with benchmark scores higher than Bakke's 549 did not make the alternates list for 1974. Thirty-two who scored higher than 549 were denied admittance to the Davis medical school. Among the whites admitted that fall, their GPAs ranged from 2.79 to 4.0. (Bakke's undergraduate GPA was 3.51.) As for the applications handled by the Task Force, the GPAs ranged from 2.21 to 3.45.

Looking at science grades, the highest GPA of a regular applicant was 4.0. The top science GPA for a Task Force applicant was 3.89. There were even wider gaps between the Medical College Admission Test (MCAT) scores of the two groups. For Bakke, these numbers would help him in his lawsuit against the "set-aside" program at Davis, where many of the applications handled by the Task Force were for students certainly "less qualified" than the soon-to-be-34-year-old aerospace engineer. Bakke had now been rejected again by the University of California, Davis, medical school. By January 1974, Allan Bakke was meeting with a lawyer.

EQUAL·JUSTICE·UNDER·LAW

6

Taking the Legal Road

The man Allan Bakke hired to represent him and his grievances in court was a "jowly, jovial man of average height and stocky build who appears a decade younger than his threescore years."[81] Having grown up in San Francisco, attorney Reynold H. Colvin called northern California his home. Colvin, known to his friends and associates as "Rennie," had graduated from Lowell High School, one of the Bay Area's more prestigious schools, then attended the University of California, Berkeley, where he graduated in 1938. He went on to Boalt Hall Law School, which was part of the Berkeley system, then went into military service during the Second World War. Following his military stint, he became an assistant

U.S. attorney. By 1951, he left public service and went into private practice.

THE "ZERO QUOTA" CASE

Colvin soon became one of San Francisco's leading attorneys. He mixed his religion and his politics. Through his involvement with the city's Jewish community, he worked as president of Temple Emanu-el, "the most influential and politically powerful synagogue in the city."[82] He was also president of the city's American Jewish Committee. By the early 1960s, Colvin was appointed by the city's mayor to hold the "Jewish seat" on the San Francisco Board of Education. Traditionally, those serving on that important urban council used it as a springboard for a career in politics. Although Colvin never used his council seat for such a move, he did make close friends and associates among the city's school administrators, as well as other officials. It was through such connections that Colvin would become involved in one of the first important cases of his legal career. In 1971, school Superintendent Thomas Shaheen, to cut school expenditures, demoted 200 San Francisco school administrators. Even as he did so, Shaheen did not include the city's small number of minority administrators in the demotions. The city had a strong affirmative action program, so Shaheen's plan would have "eliminated future advancement for white officials in the school system."[83] Outraged and frustrated, a group of white administrators hired Colvin to serve as their legal counsel. The resulting lawsuit—which became known popularly as the "Zero Quota" case—eventually landed in federal district court before Judge Joseph Conti, who was conservative on many matters, including civil rights issues. In a decision titled *Anderson v. S.F. Unified School District*, Conti ruled in favor of the suing school administrators. Although the decision did not make national headlines at the time, it would prove important for later affirmative action lawsuits, including Bakke's. Writing his decision, Judge Conti stated the following:

Preferential treatment under the guise of "affirmative action" is the imposition of one form of racial discrimination in place of another. . . . Any classification based on race is suspect: No authority exists which discriminates on racial or ethnic lines which is not being implemented to correct a prior discriminatory situation. . . . No one race or ethnic group should ever be accorded preferential treatment over another. . . . There is no place for racial groupings in America. Only in individual accomplishment can equality be achieved.[84]

As a result of the decision, the actions taken by Shaheen were reversed.

At the time, the judge's decision did not seem to have any significant implications outside of this fairly narrow employment

Although Marco DeFunis already had begun attending the law school he was suing, his case was debated by the justices of the Supreme Court. These debates would serve them well when it came time to decide *Regents of the University of California v. Bakke.*

case, but it would serve as one of the first of such decisions responding to affirmative action programs. It would also become a precedent in determining another important early case, one that Storandt had mentioned to Bakke as a case the aerospace engineer might want to look into—*DeFunis v. Odegaard.*

THE *DEFUNIS* CASE

When Storandt first mentioned the *DeFunis* case to Bakke, it was still working its way through the courts. At its center, this case was similar to what would become the *Bakke* case. It revolved around a young man who was driven and determined to see his dreams through to reality. With Marco DeFunis, however, the goal was to become a lawyer. DeFunis attended the University of Washington beginning in the late 1960s. To pay for his schooling, DeFunis worked his way through school, taking a job in a bookstore and doing manual labor for the Seattle Park Department. He graduated from the university as a Phi Beta Kappa member with a 3.62 GPA (out of a 4.0 scale), including nine hours with "A" grades in Latin. Just as Bakke would for medical school, DeFunis took an admittance exam, known as the Law Boards. He took them on three occasions before he achieved a satisfactory score of 668. His score was good enough to gain him admittance into several law schools, including those of the University of Oregon and Idaho. DeFunis, however, as a lifelong resident of Washington state, wanted to attend law school in Seattle, at the University of Washington. Just as would happen a few years later with Bakke, DeFunis applied twice and was rejected both times.

The University of Washington had a selection process that "decidedly favored minority applicants."[85] The process began with the formulation of the candidate's predicted first-year average (PFYA). This number was factored by a formula that combined the applicant's LSAT score and the grades for the candidate's junior- and senior-year undergraduate experience. Applicants having a PFYA higher than 77 typically were given admittance to the Washington system. If a candidate's score was 74.5 or below, he or she was typically rejected. DeFunis's PFYA was 76.23, which placed him in a "no-man's-land" that could result in either acceptance or rejection.

Despite this fairly structured system, the Washington system was different for applicants who were of a minority, including blacks, Hispanics, Native Americans, and Filipinos. Such candidates were admitted under a separate system, one that did not put them into direct competition with white candidates. The PFYA score was given less significance. Instead, each minority applicant's "entire record" was overviewed to determine which minority would-be student would be judged to have "the highest probability of succeeding in law school."[86] Among those candidates applying to law school for the class beginning in the fall of 1971, 37 minority students were selected. Of that number, 36 had PFYAs lower than DeFunis's 76.23, and 30 had PFYAs lower than 74.5. Save for their minority status, such candidates would not have made the cut for law school in the University of Washington system.

When he realized what had happened, a furious DeFunis decided to file a lawsuit against the university and its preferential admissions policy. Education cases related to race were certainly nothing new to the American legal system by the early 1970s. The NAACP had been sponsoring race and education cases for decades. The difference in the *DeFunis* case, however, was ironic. This time the litigant was not black or another minority. He was white.

As DeFunis's case went to court, the rejected law school applicant charged the University of Washington's law school with racial bias by allowing minorities to be admitted under a special program even though they were less qualified than he was. When the case appeared before a Washington state lower court, the court sided in favor of DeFunis. The university appealed the decision, though, and the case advanced to the Washington Supreme Court. There, the court reversed the lower court decision, decided against DeFunis, and declared that the University of Washington's admissions program was constitutional. This decision was appealed by Defunis's lawyer to the U.S. Supreme Court. The highest court in the land granted the *DeFunis* case *certiorari* (requesting records from the lower court), agreeing to hear the case. In the meantime, DeFunis began attending law school at the University of Washington, since the state's Supreme Court reversal decision was put on hold until the U.S. Supreme Court made its ruling.

In his petition to the Supreme Court, DeFunis's attorney, Josef Diamond, argued that the court should agree to hear the case, since his client's situation and its legal ramifications were concerned with two significant points of law. The first was whether the affirmative action program at the University of Washington violated the Fourteenth Amendment to the U.S. Constitution, which guarantees equal rights to all U.S. citizens, because the program appeared to give preference to racial minorities. The second was "Is Title VI of the 1964 Civil Rights Act violated because white applicants must meet different and more stringent standards than persons of other races in obtaining admissions?"[87] Diamond's question concerning Title VI of the 1964 Civil Rights Act was an important one. Under this federal law, "no program that receives federal funds can exclude anyone because of race."[88] Because the Davis medical school accepted federal dollars, Bakke's contention of admissions denial based on his race would also challenge the 1964 law.

A COMPELLING INTEREST

The briefs submitted to the Court by DeFunis's attorney made his arguments quite clear. Diamond argued that the University of Washington's law school had violated DeFunis's rights as guaranteed under the Fourteenth Amendment in two ways. The law school's policy was tilted to prefer some law school candidates "solely on the basis of race."[89] Because there were always a limited number of law school applicants accepted each year, this was a serious restriction on DeFunis's rights. In addition, the law school had established a system that judged a white candidate such as DeFunis by a higher standard than minority candidates. To this end, the university law school had not established a "compelling interest" in support of such a policy, especially if it violated the Fourteenth Amendment.[90] Diamond concluded his brief with the following summary point: "Individual rights cannot be flagrantly sacrificed in the interest of achieving racial balance. Past inequities are not corrected by creating new inequities."[91]

Although DeFunis and his lawyer were intent on having the Supreme Court agree to hear the case, officials at the University of Washington law school were just as intent that it not be heard. They believed the decision made by the Washington State Supreme Court should stand and that the school's policy should remain in place. The university's attorney, Slade Gorton, included the following question in his submitted brief: "May UWLS constitutionally take into account, as one element in selecting from among qualified candidates for the study of law, the race of applicants in pursuit of a state policy to mitigate gross under-representation of certain minorities in the law school, and in the membership of the bar?"[92] That question, in the opinion of the university law school, had already been asked and answered.

By the time the case came before the high court in early 1974, however, DeFunis was already in his third year of law school! On April 23, the Court declared the case to be moot, by a vote of 5 to 4, because DeFunis was already attending law school and would soon graduate.

Even as the court made its decision not to decide the issue but to recognize DeFunis's reality, the issue was heavily discussed among the Court's nine justices. Four of them believed that special admissions programs, such as the one in place at the University of Washington, should be addressed by a clear decision of the Court. Justice William Brennan saw the handwriting

THE ORIGINS
OF AFFIRMATIVE ACTION

The dual admissions program that the University of California, Davis, medical school had in place when Allan Bakke applied in 1973 was a fairly new program. In fact, it was based, in part, on a fairly new concept, one that was well-intentioned. Its original purpose was to right the wrongs of both the past and the present. That concept was "affirmative action."

By definition, affirmative action applies to any step, measure, or law that seeks to help minorities or women in an effort to increase their numbers in a business, organization, or school system. It is an effort to right the wrongs of the past, when women or people of a specific race or ethnic group were excluded from jobs, education systems, or representation. Affirmative action policies are established for "a larger purpose than merely breaking down the barriers and forcing compliance. Affirmative action . . . was designed to 'go out of business' by making such actions unnecessary" once the goals of the theory have been implemented by providing minorities and women new opportunities.[*]

The basic goal of affirmative action is, then, undeniably positive. By using affirmative action, for instance, a private school that had formerly been open only to whites could be opened to blacks by having the school establish a special program to encourage blacks to attend. Sometimes such a program might give blacks an advantage, such as offering them special scholarships. The school might also decide to change the admissions criteria in ways that might make blacks uniquely qualified to attend the school. Such a program might be based on the economic status of a given black population or some other criteria that recognizes the disadvantages of that group. It might be decided that some blacks who might want to attend a private school but did not qualify because of low test scores could still be admitted under an affirmative action program, because the school they attended was not adequate, making it difficult for those black students to achieve under less-than-acceptable conditions. These are certainly some of the criteria used to establish the Davis medical school Task Force.

Affirmative action had only come into practice by the late 1960s, just a few years before Allan Bakke filed his suit against the Davis medical school. Such programs had already created thousands of opportunities for women and minorities, however. The result was a more diversified work force in companies and government jobs than ever before.

Perhaps in no other field did this change make greater inroads than in the construction industry. Although white workers had dominated this industry, with affirmative action, jobs became available for many who had been shut out. The government played an important role, both on the state and federal level, by requiring construction firms who received government contracts to build roads, bridges, dams, and tunnels to hire minorities. At the same time, "set-aside" laws were passed establishing that a portion of the monies used to hire construction firms for government projects would have to go to companies owned by women or minorities.

Despite the good intentions of affirmative action programs, by the mid-1970s, many Americans were beginning to question these "set-aside" systems. Although the programs had been established to create a more level playing field for minorities and women, in order to create equality, the programs began to appear biased themselves. Affirmative action became a hot political and social topic. It should not have been surprising, then, that lawsuits such as those filed by DeFunis and Bakke were taking place.

---

* Quoted in Ron Simmons, *Affirmative Action: Conflict and Change in Higher Education After Bakke.* Cambridge, CA: Schenkman Publishing, 1982, p. 37.

Known for his liberal views, Justice William Brennan both dissented and concurred with the *Bakke* decision.

on the wall, that there was a battle going on between university affirmative action programs and those who were being "victimized" by them: "The constitutional issues which are avoided today concern vast numbers of people, organizations, and colleges and universities, as evidence by the filing of 26 amicus curiae [a Latin term meaning "friend of the court"] briefs. Few constitutional questions in recent history have stirred as much debate, and they will not disappear."[93] One of Justice William O. Douglas's law clerks (such clerks assist justices in reviewing cases and are usually well-regarded lawyers them-selves) may have summed up the meaning of the Court's re-sponse even more accurately: "I think it would be fairly obvious that all the court is doing is ducking the issue."[94]

The concerns and predictions of Justice Brennan that the Court would not see an end to affirmative action cases beyond *DeFunis* were almost immediately proven true. Just days after the Court's April 1974 decision rendering the *DeFunis* case moot (or having no further point), Allan Bakke was on the phone to his attorney, Reynold Colvin. He generally had but one impor-tant question for Colvin: "Well," asked Bakke, "what are you go-ing to do for me now?"[95]

EQUAL·JUSTICE·UNDER·LAW·

7

A Filing for Bakke

Despite the Court's *DeFunis* rendering, Bakke believed he had a case. There was, after all, the decision in *Anderson v. S.F. Unified School District,* which had been decided against affirmative action in the San Francisco school system. Bakke's potential lawsuit and legal situation was not exactly the same as that of the San Francisco school administrators who had sued the system, however. The school case had involved public decisions. Bakke was only aware of the Davis medical school's policy of set asides through a clandestine meeting with a school official. The San Francisco decision concerned school officials who had a vested interest—those who had a clear stake in the changes it brought about. Bakke had not been a clear and purposeful target of the Davis application policy. He would have to prove, if he decided to sue, that he had been victimized personally, specifically. He had to establish something the legal system refers to as "standing." In other words, Bakke "had to prove not only that there was a quota for minority students but that he had been injured by this quota."[96] He would have to prove as best he could that, if there had been no Task Force and no alleged preferential admissions policy, he would have been admitted to the Davis medical school.

A CASE IN YOLO COUNTY

If Bakke was going to file a lawsuit, its timing was going to be crucial. Bakke had wanted to be admitted to medical school for the fall semester of 1974. Any court case would still be in process by that time. Bakke knew about the specifics of *DeFunis*, however. A judge had ordered the University of Washington to admit DeFunis to its law school even though the case was still working its way through the legal system. Bakke's lawyer instructed his client to try the same thing. Colvin told Bakke to take his case to the Superior Court in Yolo County, California, the same county where the medical school was located. There, Colvin hoped to argue his case before a state court judge, one who knew about the Davis-based university as a local judge, one who could look at Bakke's case in real terms. Any other judge, one removed from the immediate regional situation might only view the case in the abstract and hold Bakke out of school until the legal process had run its course. Colvin's logic made sense. As he described his client's situation: "While [Bakke] had no constitutional right to be in medical school, he did have the constitutional right not to be discriminated against. From our point of view, he was there as an individual."[97] Bakke agreed to his lawyer's legal strategy.

In taking this approach, however, Colvin was deciding not to pursue his client's case as a class action suit. In such cases, a lawyer files a case technically on behalf of an entire group of people, not just one client. Bakke could be presented in court

Allan Bakke filed his complaint at the Yolo County, California, courthouse.

to a judge as an individual, one with a face and a name. Colvin could present Allan Bakke—"Vietnam veteran, aerospace engineer, and a man with a strong commitment to medicine"—not just another embittered, disappointed white man. Soon, Colvin's approach paid off for Bakke.[98]

Despite these plans, Colvin did approach university officials one last time before filing his client's suit, to see if they were willing to reconsider admitting Bakke. If they would allow Bakke to enter the fall of 1974 class, the suit would be dropped. For a time, Davis officials considered granting Bakke's request. It might allow them to swing clear of a complicated legal battle. In the end, however, the offer was rejected. The university was too concerned that, if they made an exception with Bakke, they might set precedent: They might open themselves up to other requests from other candidates they had also rejected.

Bakke's attorney filed his complaint on June 20, 1974, just two months following the Supreme Court's *DeFunis* decision. The complaint was filed in Yolo's county seat, the town of Woodland. The filing and the requisite papers were short and to the point, nothing more than four pages explaining the case and an additional page that was an affidavit signed by Bakke that everything he contended was true to the best of his knowledge. There were no television cameras or fanfare. Colvin went about his business methodically, almost quietly. Within the complaint, Colvin stated the case succinctly, claiming that his client was "and is in all respects duly qualified for admission to [the Davis] Medical School and the sole reason his application was rejected was on account of his race, to-wit, Caucasian and white, and not for reasons applicable to persons of every race."[99]

Colvin was specific in stating whom he held responsible for Bakke's rejection from the Davis medical school. He mentioned the school's Task Force:

> a special admissions committee composed of racial minority members [that had] evaluated applications of a special group of persons purportedly from economic and educationally disadvantaged backgrounds; that from this group, a quota of 16 percent, or 16 out of 100 first-year class members, was selected; that, in fact, all applicants admitted to said medical school as members of this group were members of racial minorities, that under this admission program racial minority and majority applicants went through separate segregated admission procedures with separate standards for admissions; that the use of such separate standards resulted in the admission of minority applicants less qualified than plaintiff and other nonminority applicants who were therefore rejected.[100]

In his filed brief, Colvin argued that Bakke's rights had been violated by the actions of Davis medical school officials as guaranteed by California's state constitution, the Fourteenth

Amendment to the U.S. Constitution, and Title VI of the Civil Rights Act of 1964.

THE UNIVERSITY RESPONDS

Davis officials would not respond to Bakke's filed complaint against the medical school for 33 days. The University of California was a gigantic institution, which, in the mid-1970s, comprised nine separate campuses, from Davis in northern California down to San Diego near the state's southern border. Nearly 10,000 people worked for the immense education system, and its student enrollment exceeded 120,000. The state university system had been created under the California Constitution as an independent entity, although it was dependent on the state legislature in Sacramento, the state capital, for much of its funding. This sprawling system was directed by the University Board of Regents, comprising elected officials as well as private citizens appointed by the state's governor. Despite its tremendous scope, breadth, and dimension, in 1974, the entire multicampus system relied on a cadre of 18 full-time lawyers, an average of two per campus.

When Colvin sent a copy of his brief to the university (the same day he filed the brief with the court in Woodland), it was delivered to the university's general counsel office, located in University Hall on the University of California, Berkeley, campus, "a dull, colorless blockhouse of concrete, glass, and brick that serves as the administrative center for the entire system."[101] The brief was soon in the hands of the supervising attorney for the University of California system, Donald L. Reidhaar. It was a position he had held for less than a year.

Reidhaar had spent his entire law career up and down the Pacific Coast. He had graduated from the University of Washington (the same system DeFunis had recently sued) in 1957 with a business degree. He then attended Boalt Hall, the law school at the University of California, Berkeley. After receiving his law degree, he served as a clerk to an Oregon Supreme Court justice.

Reidhaar moved to San Francisco in 1961 and went into private practice with the law firm of Pillsbury, Madison, and Sutro. After working there just under a year, he took a position with the University of California's legal office, where he worked for nearly a decade as an assistant counsel. He made associate counsel and, by 1973, had been appointed as the university's top lawyer.

When Reidhaar's office received its copy of Bakke's filed suit, the university was disunited on the issue of affirmative action. It was not that the university had not had earlier complaints lodged against its admissions policies, both from individuals and organized groups, but the university had never been faced with legal action. When the *DeFunis* case was still in the court system, University of California officials had watched with a close eye, hoping that a Supreme Court decision would provide them with some direction and guidelines they could develop for the entire university system. That, in fact, was the problem. University officials had never created a uniform, umbrella system for its nine campuses regarding affirmative action. Individual campuses had always been free to develop their own policies, standards, and guidelines on this issue. This had resulted in a crazy quilt of different policies, all practiced within the university system. This placed the university in an awkward position when Bakke decided to sue. The appearance was that the university had not taken the issue seriously, had not worked up a uniform policy, and had no real direction regarding affirmative action. In later legal documents created as the Bakke case wound its way through the courts, Reidhaar and his colleagues tried to explain the different policies as an attempt by the university to allow "autonomy on the individual campuses."[102]

Even as the university appeared ill-prepared to meet a lawsuit such as Bakke's, though, Reidhaar's response was quiet and understated. He handed it off to three of his staff lawyers. These attorneys made a trip to the Davis medical school and interviewed several of the school's staff and officials, including the dean of admissions, George Lowrey; the chair of the school's

Task Force, Dr. Lindy Kumagai, the medical school dean, Dr. C. John Tupper; and Peter Storandt, who had already shared so much information concerning the school's admissions policy with Bakke. As for Storandt, he was somewhat relieved to find that Bakke had, indeed, decided to sue. He thought such a suit would be beneficial for the Davis-based medical school:

> We believed it was going to be a strictly social issue. It was going to be one of those precedent-setting decisions that would help the medical school devise a better program and maintain its commitment to minority education. Maybe we were optimistic and idealistic and maybe all of these things.[103]

From the beginning, however, it seems the case did not appear to be unfolding as university officials hoped. The university attorneys did not seem to know exactly what questions to ask. To those they interviewed, they appeared overly confident. After his interview, Dr. Kumagai "thought at least one of the lawyers was 'overtly against affirmative action.'"[104]

MISTAKES ALONG THE WAY

There was no reason for any of the university lawyers to be overly confident. The Bakke suit had real merit, and many within the university, especially those associated with the medical school, knew it. There was no question that the medical school admissions policy separated out applications into two piles, one regular and the other special and delivered to the Task Force. It was a matter of fact that those on the two admissions committees interviewed candidates and ranked them before submitting recommendations to the full admissions committee. It was also a fact that in the years the Task Force had selected candidates, the committee had never selected a white applicant as a "disadvantaged" candidate. The subcommittee had, indeed, interviewed white applicants, but had not selected one. This, however, was information never presented to the university's legal team.

The university's legal team also failed to collect all the information they should have had in creating the university's defense against the Bakke suit. They chose to center their defense on the information they gained from Dr. Lowrey, the admissions dean. Unfortunately, Lowrey had no first-hand knowledge of the workings of the Task Force because he had never worked with the subcommittee directly. The university's lawyers also failed to take a stand against Bakke's claim that the university's medical school admissions policy operated under a quota system. In fact, the school's lawyers, early on, "conceded that a quota was in operation by submitting statistics showing that in each year Bakke applied, 16 students were admitted through the Task Force."[105] They were not aware for a long time that, in 1974, the Task Force only selected 15 candidates for admission, choosing to hand back the sixteenth opening to the regular committee, because the Task Force didn't think it had a qualified sixteenth minority candidate. Such information might have assisted the school's attorneys. They could have argued that the "quota" system was not that rigid and that it did not admit "unqualified applicants," as Bakke's suit contended.

Another mistake made by the university's legal team was its failure to reveal that middle-class, minority candidates were typically referred to the regular committee for consideration and that the regular committee denied admission to minority applicants who were well-qualified. According to Dr. Kumagai, "They would say he or she only has a 3.4 [GPA] instead of a 3.6. I would point out that they were accepting whites with 3.4 and much less."[106]

In addition, Reidhaar and his colleagues did not present information on another admissions "policy" used at the Davis medical school. During these same years, medical school Dean Tupper had made a regular practice of intervening in the admissions process by admitting students of wealthy and influential patrons and supporters of the school. Tupper did not inform the school's attorneys of this and only admitted it to a Davis newspaper after the

THE YOLO COURT AND
A RETIRED JUDGE

When Allan Bakke decided to take his case to court in 1974, his attorney, Reynold H. Colvin, insisted that the case be presented to a lower California court. Bakke's attorney had his reasons. Colvin wanted the case to appear in a court in close geographical proximity to the University of California, Davis. That way, the case would be heard by a judge who would probably have at least some firsthand knowledge concerning the Davis campus and could look at the case from a closer angle than a judge who might be removed from the San Francisco region. The Yolo County Courthouse became Colvin's destination.

The courthouse was situated in the county seat of Woodland. At that time, one could take State Highway 113 out of Woodland to Interstate 80 and reach the Davis campus in a matter of minutes. The Davis campus was only 11 miles out of Woodland. The town is located in the Sacramento Valley, in a part of California that, in the mid-1970s, looked more like a small town in the Midwest than one located in the bustling metropolitan region dominated by San Francisco. Farm fields surrounded Woodland, a rural landscape dotted by grain elevators, where, during the long hot summers, farmers worked their fields using the latest mechanized farm equipment to bring in great harvests of tomatoes, sugar beets, corn, and soybeans. It was agricultural work that had gone on around Woodland for an unbroken century. The farms featured great old Victorian houses, furthering the illusion that Woodland was part of another Midwestern world. The occasional palm trees were the only giveaway that the farm region was in California.

Woodland itself was a busy community of 25,000 residents, an otherwise unnoticeable town "complete with its Main Street and a handful of stores touting everything from farm equipment to consumer goods."* The town and Yolo County had a colorful history that included Spanish missionary-explorers who had reached the valley in 1817 and found local Indians, the Patwin. The Patwin lived by hunting the abundance of local game, including salmon, deer, and the tule elk, which is today extinct. Spanish ranchers followed; one ranch was established by a wealthy citizen of San Francisco, Francisco Guerrero y Palomares. Gold prospectors had tromped across the county by the 1850s, with most finding little gold.

A town sprang up, Woodland, and prospered during the last decades of the nineteenth century. By the 1890s, Woodland had become a thriving agricultural community with its own railroad station. Even though a great fire swept through the town in 1892, Woodland continued on into the twentieth century. Having never lost its small-town atmosphere and peaceful pace, the community had remained home to a mixed population of whites, blacks, and Latinos.

Even as this quiet northern California town's courthouse became the center stage for a legal battle that would come to have national consequences, it did not stir up the local population. When Colvin filed Bakke's case in Woodland's court, the local court clerks became excited, not because it was going to bring attention to their court and their town; instead, they viewed the case as "a welcome break from the normal routine of minor civil suits and domestic disputes."[**]

Ironically, when the *Bakke* case was filed at the Yolo County Courthouse, the two sitting judges were both so busy with their own backlog of cases that neither had the time to hear the case. Sixty-seven-year-old Judge F. Leslie Manker would have to be called out of retirement to sit on the bench and give Bakke's case its hearing. Manker had stepped down from the court five years earlier.

[*] Quoted in Ron Simmons, *Affirmative Action: Conflict and Change in Higher Education After Bakke.* Cambridge, CA: Schenkman Publishing, 1982, p. 56.
[**] Ibid., p. 57.

case had appeared before the California Supreme Court. The dean stated that he had "intervened hundreds of times" in this way. One such example involved the daughter-in-law of one of the university's former chancellors. Another was on behalf of the son of B. Kent Wilson, a former president of the Medical Society of Yolo County. There had been a special admission of the "sons of the state senator and assemblyman who headed finance committees responsible for the medical school budget."[107] Sometimes such students might not even be interviewed at all, but simply admitted. Such information would have been extremely valuable in the university's defense.

Perhaps the university's lawyers made another error in the way they approached the *Bakke* lawsuit. Attorney Reidhaar decided to meet Bakke's assertions by claiming that, special admissions program aside, Bakke would not have been admitted to the University of California, Davis, medical school anyway. After all, he argued, 32 applicants with scores higher than Bakke's had also been turned down, and all of them were white. Reidhaar also approached the *Bakke* case with a broader agenda. He was prepared to go to court not just to answer whether the white aerospace engineer should be allowed admission to the Davis medical school. He wanted the court to decide that the university's admissions policy was acceptable, legal, and constitutional. To make his point, Reidhaar filed a cross complaint to the court that explained the extreme competitiveness of admittance to the Davis medical school, as well as the reasoning behind the school using race in selecting as least a portion of its students.

FORMING THEIR CASES

As for Bakke's attorney, Colvin met with Dr. Lowrey on July 23 at University Hall for an interview. Attorney Reidhaar was present at that meeting. It was then that Colvin gained full access to the Davis medical school's files, Bakke's application folder, and all the statistical evidence comparing the regular applicants against the Task Force applicants. Colvin grilled Lowrey for information, asking him to go "through a step-by-step explanation of the selection process at Davis: the separation of files into 'disadvantaged' and regular groups; elimination of regular applicants below the 2.5 GPA; the interview process; and the method of grading according to benchmark scores."[108] During his interview with Lowrey, Colvin stayed focused on the statistical information and the differences between scores of Task Force and regular students. Some Task Force students were admitted with grades below the 2.5 benchmark for regular students. In fact, Colvin noted that with one class, the gap between the average of the two groups was almost a full point—3.36 for regular applicants and 2.42 for Task Force applicants. Lowrey could only agree there was a serious difference.

As both sides collected data and information on which they would establish their cases, the date for the start of the fall semester of 1974 was swiftly approaching. Bakke still wanted to be among those who started classes at the medical school. His attorney approached Reidhaar in hopes of coming up with a solution to the situation short of a protracted legal battle. His hope was that the school would allow Bakke to enroll while the legal process ran its course. Colvin told Reidhaar that "Allan Bakke belongs in medical school. He should have been admitted in the first place." If the school simply admitted his client to the fall 1974 semester, "There will be no more lawsuit, and since there are no other plaintiffs in this case, it will be over."[109] From the university's point of view, enrolling Bakke and ending his suit would certainly buy the university system time to prepare more adequately for another lawsuit, one that was bound to show up sooner or later. Reidhaar, however, on behalf of the school, turned down Colvin's offer. There are indications that Reidhaar and his team, as well as university officials, were not yet taking the *Bakke* case that seriously. In July, Reidhaar met with the regents of the state university system, a meeting that

Conservative economist and political writer Thomas Sowell is an outspoken opponent of affirmative action. Bakke's attorney quoted Sowell in his arguments.

produced no alarm bells for the school administrators. *Bakke* was simply viewed as "just another lawsuit before a lower court, and few could have guessed the impact it would have in just a few months."[110]

The court case continued. During the first week of August 1974, Colvin appeared in court and presented his first legal argument, calling for the university to admit his client. Colvin appeared before Judge F. Leslie Manker, a retired judge who was brought in to hear the case, as the court's two sitting judges were handling too many cases already. Colvin noted that Bakke had been denied admission on two occasions, despite his GPA and his MCAT scores, even though they were "both high and in fact higher than those of some who were admitted."[111] Colvin further argued that Bakke's rejection, based on racial set asides, constituted a violation of his rights under the equal protection clause of the Fourteenth Amendment. As Colvin stated things, Bakke had only been rejected from admission to the Davis medical school based on his race and the race of those selected by the Task Force. If Bakke had been a member of some other racial minority, he would have been admitted based on his scores, and a denial would have violated the constitution. Colvin also mentioned in his presentation the opinions of a black professor at UCLA, Thomas Sowell, an outspoken critic of affirmative action. Using Sowell's words, Colvin argued that "Task Force students were being labeled as incapable of meeting the higher standards of admission applied to non-minority candidates."[112]

A LEGAL DECISION

Reidhaar and other university lawyers took nearly a month to respond to Colvin's presentation before Manker. It would be Reidhaar's position that Bakke's denial of admission was not based on the school's affirmative action policy. He would have been denied admission even through the regular system, as he had been. Reidhaar contended that the medical school's admission policy was fair. In his words, "The special admissions program is designed to serve the legitimate needs of the Davis Medical School, the medical profession, and society."[113] The university's lead counsel also argued that the school's policy was constitutional: "The question is whether the Constitution is to deny members of minority groups from disadvantaged backgrounds the kind of preference which is routinely granted to a myriad other individuals and groups."[114]

Three weeks following the presentation of the university's defense, Colvin was back before Judge Manker, responding to the university's arguments. He observed that the university had not yet made the argument that any minority students handled by the Task Force had actually been better qualified for admission to the Davis school than Bakke. He noted that the university had basically already admitted to the use of a racial quota system. He stated that the university had not presented adequate proof that Bakke would not have been admitted even without the Task Force and the 16-student set aside. It was during Colvin's presentation on August 24 that he would use the term "reverse discrimination" for the first time in court. When Reidhaar's turn before the judge came next, he continued to argue that the university policy was fair and that the motives behind it were well-intended: to provide a greater level of opportunity for disadvantaged minority students.

Following this flurry of presentations before Judge Manker, the date was set for a hearing—September 27—concerning Bakke's request to be admitted to the Davis medical school for the fall semester. During the hearing, the only people present were Bakke and Colvin at one table, Reidhaar and his support attorneys at another, and those observing the proceedings: Dr. Lowrey and Bakke's wife, who held their three-year-old daughter. During his presentation before the judge, Colvin emphasized the same arguments he had presented previously concerning test scores and other data. Reidhaar re-emphasized Lowrey's insistence that the Task Force made its decisions by looking closely at a variety of factors, not just grades and test scores. He reminded Judge Manker that the Davis medical school policy made significant connections between an applicant's race and his or her "economic or educational disadvantage."[115]

The only surprise during the hearing came when Colvin, near the end of the court session, made an offer to the university's lawyers that he would accept the judge's decision on the hearing and waive a full-blown trial. It was a bold step, a serious gamble, but Bakke wanted to get the proceedings over, hoping the judge would rule in his favor, admitting him to the Davis program, and the aerospace engineer would be on his way to attaining the medical degree he so desperately wanted. The offer was so attractive to Reidhaar that he accepted, completely forgetting to make his argument before the judge concerning his cross complaint he had filed requesting the judge to rule on the Davis policy's constitutionality.

8

Notice of Intended Decision

Despite Reynold Colvin's tactic to have a trial waived, the judge did not issue a decision immediately. Consequently, Allan Bakke was not able to enter the fall 1974 class at the University of California, Davis. In fact, Judge Manker did not actually make a decision until November. On the November 25, the judge filed a "Notice of Intended Decision." Using the *DeFunis* decision and the earlier Colvin case, *Anderson v. S.F. Unified School District*, the judge decided with Bakke that he had been denied admission to the Davis school even though he was a qualified applicant. The judge, however, did not agree that Bakke had proven that he "had a right to be in the medical school."[116]

In addition, Manker ruled that the University of California, Davis, medical school's special admissions program, embodied in the Task Force, was not constitutional. The policy rested on a quota system, which allowed minority candidates to compete against one another for 16 seats, while not competing against the other candidates chosen under the regular admissions policy. In Manker's words, "No race or ethnic group should ever be granted privileges or immunities not given to every other race."[117] To further his point, Manker quoted from the chief justice of the Washington Supreme Court, Frank Hale, in his dissent written for the *DeFunis* decision: "Racial bigotry, prejudice and intolerance will never be ended by exalting the political rights of one group or class over that of another. The circle of inequality cannot be broken by shifting the inequities from one man to his neighbor."[118]

"BOTH SIDES LOST"

As it turned out, Manker's decision did not completely satisfy either side. Yes, Bakke's case had led a state judge to determine that the Davis medical school's special and dual admissions policy was not legal. On the other hand, Bakke's true desire, to be admitted to the medical school, had not been satisfied. Attorney Colvin would sum up the judge's decision by noting, "What happened at Woodland was that both sides lost."[119]

Although the university would emerge from the decision with disappointment, they would be even more disappointed in the months that followed. Following Manker's initial decision, one that was still in its early stages, the judge asked both sides to give their responses. When Colvin subsequently argued that the university medical school's special admissions program be ended, a request he had never made previously, Manker agreed. He issued his final ruling on the *Bakke* case on March 7, 1975. In this, the judge also changed another crucial part of his decision:

He issued an order that prohibited Davis from using race as any kind of factor in admissions, and he also shifted the burden of proof in Bakke's case to the university. Instead of Bakke having to prove that he *would* have gotten in if there were no task force, the school now had to prove that he would *not* have been admitted.[120]

ON TO THE CALIFORNIA SUPREME COURT

With neither side satisfied with Judge Manker's decision, both Colvin and Reidhaar technically joined forces, if only to take the case to the next level. (Following Manker's March 1975 ruling, Reidhaar offered to have Bakke's application for the fall 1976 medical school term reviewed, but he clearly hinted that the application would be reviewed just as any other "coming in at this late date."[121] His message was clear: Bakke should not take the possibility of his being admitted too seriously, thus ensuring that Bakke would want to continue taking his case through the legal system.) Two months later, both lawyers requested that the California Supreme Court agree to hear the case of *University of California Regents v. Bakke*. By June 26, 1975, the justices on the state's highest court agreed. They understood that the *Bakke* case was an important one that focused on an issue of national significance. The *Bakke* case was "no longer a local matter before a local judge."[122]

By appealing to the California Supreme Court, the university was advancing its strategy. It wanted the case to be heard by a court with a progressive reputation. This was certainly the case with the California Supreme Court. The court was known for its liberal decisions regarding the death penalty, protections for the poor, and safeguards for civil and constitutional rights, including sex discrimination. The state's high court, during the mid-1970s, was certainly more liberal than the U.S. Supreme Court at that time. Many legal experts expected the California Supreme Court to decide in favor of the university and strike a statewide blow that would favor affirmative action.

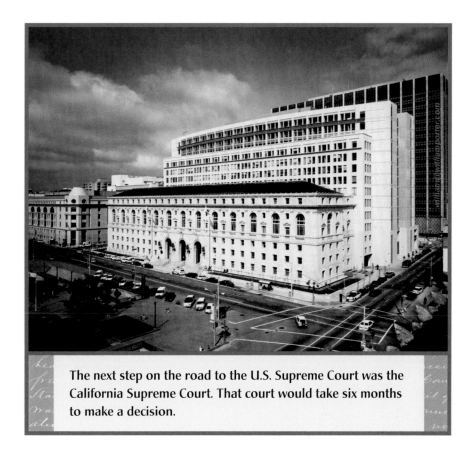

The next step on the road to the U.S. Supreme Court was the California Supreme Court. That court would take six months to make a decision.

Once the California Supreme Court agreed to look at the *Bakke* case, other interested parties came forward, each interested in the court's potential decision. Several groups immediately filed *amicus curiae* briefs. Because the Bakke case was, at least in part, based on race and racial preferences, the case could impact affirmative action programs across America. The "friends of the court" that filed such briefs included the National Urban League and the NAACP Legal Defense and Educational Fund, both black organizations; the Asian American Bar Association; the Puerto Rican Legal Defense and Education Fund; various law schools; the Fair Employment Practice Commission of California; the American Association of University Professors; and various universities, including

Harvard, Stanford, Rutgers, the University of Pennsylvania, and the University of Washington. Several filed their briefs in support of the university. Others, such as the Anti-Defamation

 TWO JEWISH JUSTICES

When the California Supreme Court decided the *Bakke* case, the court voted six to one against the university's affirmative policy. Among the justices were two of Jewish descent—Mathew Tobriner and Stanley Mosk. But the two men did not agree in their decision in the *Bakke* case. One voted with the majority and the other cast the lone dissent. The two serve as a study in contrasts in their opinions concerning the *Bakke* case.

The two justices had several things in common. Both had been appointed by the same California governor, Edmund "Pat" Brown—Tobriner in 1962 and Mosk two years later. During their shared decade on the California Supreme Court, Tobriner and Mosk had become fast friends. They had both lived in California most of their lives, were known as shrewd legal experts, and both had reputations as liberal justices.

They were different men in other ways, however. Mosk had grown up in a middle-class home during the Great Depression, his father struggling to run a small business. Mosk attended law school in Illinois, where he had to work to help support himself at a job that paid $7.50 a week. After graduation, Mosk, eager and young, left for Southern California, looking for a job as a lawyer. Through the years, he became a judge known for his support of civil rights. He later became California attorney general, where he continued his fight against segregation, a struggle he had continued from the bench as a justice on the state's highest court. His views on civil rights had not stopped him from deciding in Bakke's favor, though. In Mosk's words: "In this case we confront a sensitive and complex issue: whether a special admission program . . . offends the constitutional rights of better qualified applicants denied admission because they are not identified with a minority."* Mosk had decided that such a program was not acceptable.

League of B'nai B'rith, the American Jewish Congress, and the American Federation of Teachers, filed in support of Bakke and against using racial quotas. The *Bakke* case was shaping up

As for Tobriner, he had grown up in an upper-class family "in a magnificent Victorian house built by his father right after the 1906 earthquake."** In the mid-1970s, Tobriner still lived in the old family house. He had attended Stanford, followed by Harvard Law School. After graduation, he came back to the Bay Area, where he worked with labor unions and farm cooperatives, representing them in cases involving labor law. He practiced that field of law for nearly 30 years, until 1959. During that time, he became friends with Edmund Brown, who would one day become the state's governor. (Along the way, Brown and Tobriner both switched their support from the Republican Party to the Democrats largely due to their support and respect for President Franklin Roosevelt.)

After Brown became governor in 1959, he first offered his friend a seat on the California Court of Appeals; then, two years later, Brown selected Tobriner for the California Supreme Court. During the court's discussions on the *Bakke* case, Tobriner had argued his side admirably despite being outnumbered. In his words: "I argued very loudly and long and strenuously, but as you know, I received no other vote."***

Tobriner's dissent was a 57-page document. In it, he stated his opinion that it was sad that Bakke's lawyer was using the Fourteenth Amendment as a means of "preventing graduate schools from voluntarily integrating."† In the end, however, his voice would not be heard by his colleagues on the California Supreme Court.

* Quoted in Joel Dreyfuss and Charles Lawrence III. *The Bakke Case: The Politics of Inequality.* New York: Harcourt Brace Jovanovich, 1979, p. 74.
** Ibid., p. 72.
*** Ibid., p. 73
† Quoted in Rebecca Stefoff, *The Bakke Case: Challenging Affirmative Action.* New York: Marshall Cavendish, 2006, p. 82.

as an important case with many interested parties watching the legal proceedings with anxious eyes.

BEFORE THE CALIFORNIA HIGH COURT

Briefs for both sides were filed with the California Supreme Court on March 18, 1976. Generally, the legal strategies of both the university and of Bakke had not fundamentally changed, so the content of the briefs was largely the same as had been filed in Superior Court in Yolo County before Judge Manker. Attorney Colvin was still claiming that Bakke's rights had been violated by the university's medical school admissions policy, rights guaranteed him under the equal protection clause of the Fourteenth Amendment to the U.S. Constitution. He also claimed the policy was a violation of California law and of the Civil Rights Act of 1964.

Colvin also contended that, according to precedents already established by earlier court cases, racial discrimination was only allowable "in remedial situations."[123] This meant that the University of California, Davis, medical school's policy of race-based admissions was only allowable as a means of trying to correct past wrongs. Because the university medical school had never intentionally used the dual admissions policy to purposefully harm someone or some group, its policy could not continue to be allowed. University attorney Reidhaar, however, countered that "there was a difference between programs instituted to assist minorities and those which discriminated against them."[124] He also argued, as he had in the Yolo County Court, that Bakke, even without the affirmative action program at Davis, "was so far from acceptance . . . he would have been rejected."[125]

The seven justices on the California Supreme Court took six months to render their decision in the *Bakke* case. The September decision was an instantaneous surprise to many legal experts and other observers. A majority of six decided to uphold Judge Manker's earlier decision that Davis's medical school

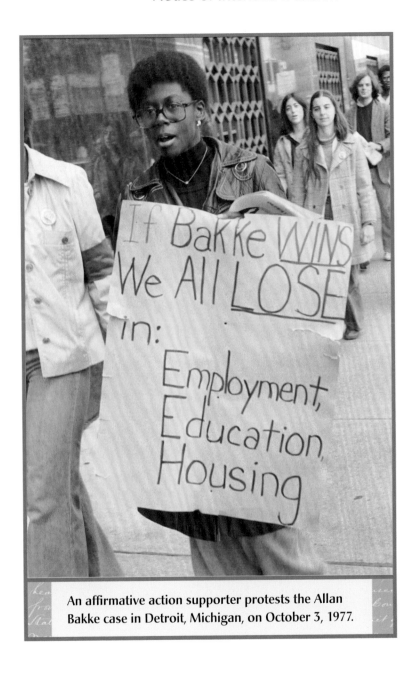

An affirmative action supporter protests the Allan
Bakke case in Detroit, Michigan, on October 3, 1977.

admissions policy was, in fact, based on racial quotas and was
thus illegal. With the court responding largely to the same evidence, testimony, and statistics that had been presented to the
Manker court, the high court's ruling had a familiar sound to it:

We conclude that the program . . . violates the constitutional rights of nonminority applicants because it affords preference on the basis of race to persons who, by the University's own standards, are not as qualified for the study of medicine as nonminority applicants denied admission."[126]

The court's only dissenter was a Jewish justice, Mathew Tobriner. (Another justice of Jewish heritage on the court was Stanley Mosk, who had voted in favor of Bakke.) In his dissent, Tobriner stated that, in his opinion, "the majority incorrectly asserts that the minority students accepted under the special admission program are 'less qualified'—under the medical school's own standards—than nonminority applicants rejected by the medical school. This simply is not the case."[127]

In rendering its decision, the California Supreme Court had agreed that Bakke's rights as guaranteed under the Fourteenth Amendment had been violated. The court, however, declined to state that the university's policy was a violation of California law or the 1964 Civil Rights Act, as Colvin had argued. In addition to this decision, the state Supreme Court told the university to return to Judge Manker's court in Yolo County "to determine if Bakke would have been admitted in the absence of the special admissions program."[128] In the weeks that followed, when university medical school officials failed to prove that Bakke's application would have been rejected even without the special admissions policy and the Task Force, the majority of the California Supreme Court amended their ruling and, on October 28, 1976, ordered the Davis-based medical school to admit Allan Bakke to the school's program. Bakke's dream of attending medical school seemed closer than ever to becoming reality.

EQUAL·JUSTICE·UNDER·LAW·

"I Am Allan Bakke's Attorney"

9

Despite the October ruling in his favor by the California Supreme Court, Bakke soon found his way to the University of California, Davis, School of Medicine blocked yet again.

Just two weeks after the state court's ruling to allow Bakke to enroll at the Davis campus, Reidhaar appeared before the court requesting a stay of the court's order for 30 days to give the university time to decide whether it would appeal. The California Supreme Court did the university one better. They agreed to stay their decision indefinitely if the U.S. Supreme Court decided to hear the case. Four days later, the university's regents voted 11 to 1 to take the *Bakke* case to the highest court in the land. Even as they did so, they were being besieged by civil rights groups across the country not to take the case further. If the liberal California Supreme Court had not decided in favor of the university's affirmative action program, there was a lesser possibility that the more conservative court in Washington would so do.

NEW COURT, NEW ATTORNEYS

Reidhaar enthusiastically supported the decision of the regents to take the case to the high court. He had always favored that option to establish, once and for all, the constitutionality of the Davis medical school admissions policy. Reidhaar claimed he and his team had a good probability of winning the university's case. To increase that likelihood, Reidhaar brought in a new attorney from outside the university's stable: Paul Mishkin, a law professor at the University of California, Berkeley, and an expert in constitutional law.

By December 14, 1976, Reidhaar and his associates had filed the first brief with the high court, a *writ of certiorari*, and asking that the court agree to hear the case as soon as possible. Simultaneously, a host of groups who were opposed to the university taking the case to the Supreme Court filed their own briefs asking the high court to deny the university's appeal. These groups included the National Organization for Women, the National Urban League, and the National Conference of Black Lawyers. There were those who did not believe the university attorneys had pursued the case with enough enthusiasm and thoroughness. As for Reidhaar, he resented such accusations: "If [*Bakke*] is an example of someone trying to lose a case, I don't know how the hell you go about winning one."[129]

Critics, especially in various minority communities, did not feel the university's case was the right one to take to the high court as a test of affirmative action. The university had no history of discrimination that could validate an affirmative action program. The policy at the medical school was, as two courts had already determined, an outright quota system. Bakke was "a model plaintiff whose objective qualifications far outshone those of minority [students at Davis]."[130] Among those who did not want the case to move on to the U.S. Supreme Court was Bakke's attorney, Reynold Colvin. He filed a brief with the court asking that a *writ of certiorari* not be issued to hear the case, because, he argued, the California Supreme Court decision should be allowed to stand.

Through December 1976, and January 1977, the justices on the U.S. Supreme Court discussed the case, well aware of the large number of constituencies opposed to their hearing it. The anxious critics were disappointed, however, when, on February 22, 1977, the Supreme Court agreed to give a hearing to the case titled *Regents of the University of California v. Allan Bakke.* Four years had passed since Allan Bakke had applied to the University of California, Davis, School of Medicine. In some ways, the case had moved past him. It was no longer about a white, 30-something, aerospace engineer from California. It was about an issue—affirmative action—and its future role in the American educational system.

Even before the justices of the U.S. Supreme Court heard the *Bakke* case, the controversy surrounding it was becoming an ever-widening circle. Following the California Supreme Court decision, 2,000 people gathered to protest in San Francisco's Civic Center Plaza. The news media was covering every square inch of the story. The number of briefs filed by "friends of the court" reached an all-time high. In all, 58 *amici curiae* briefs were presented to the Supreme Court; they represented an incredible 160 interested parties and individuals. Those included a variety of organizations, including the American Bar Association, the NAACP, the American Civil Liberties Union, Americans for Democratic Action, and the National Education Association; and elite universities, such as Columbia, Harvard, the University of Pennsylvania, and Stanford. Briefs in support of Bakke were also filed, including those by several

Jewish groups. Among those briefs was one filed on behalf of the Young Americans for Freedom. The Seattle attorney who filed the brief was Marco DeFunis.

BEFORE THE COURT

Although the Supreme Court justices agreed in February 1977 to hear the *Bakke* case, it would not come before them for eight months, on Columbus Day, October 12. (The U.S. Supreme Court takes up cases each fall in October.) The day of the hearing before the court, people lined up outside the Supreme Court building to witness history. Some had been waiting beneath the Court's great marble pillars since 4 A.M. There were so many wanting to witness the proceedings that day that Court officials decided to rotate people in and out of the courtroom, giving each group only three minutes to observe the hearing. Inside the courtroom, the scene and stage was being set:

> Even as the crowds waited, Court employees placed ten-inch quill pens on writing pads at the counsel tables in the courtroom. All these gestures were in keeping with the image of tradition promoted by the 16 Corinthian columns of the Court's façade, the black robes of the justices, and the red velvet curtains around the courtroom's perimeter. The mystique of tradition and formality gave the Court its power, and this power was guarded jealously.[131]

At 9:30 A.M., the guards in the Court building began allowing spectators to enter. Each passed through a metal detector. Meanwhile, across the street from the Supreme Court, hundreds of demonstrators had gathered, many carrying signs and banners in support of either the university or Bakke.

In a short time, the attorneys for both sides appeared. Reidhaar was present, alongside Archibald Cox. Paul Mishkin had been instrumental in preparing the university's brief. Cox, a prominent Harvard law professor, had been selected to

Demonstrators protest the *Bakke* decision in Oakland, California, on October 8, 1977.

present the case before the Supreme Court. Cox was a well-known national figure. He had served as a special prosecutor during the Watergate scandal in 1973, which would the following year result in the resignation of President Richard Nixon. Colvin had remained Bakke's attorney, although the aerospace engineer had spent all the money he could afford to pay him. Colvin, along with an associate, Robert Links, however, were now representing Bakke for free. Also in the room, taking their places along one of the long tables in front of the long, raised mahogany bench where the justices sat, were a pair of government lawyers: Wade McCree, the U.S. solicitor general, and Drew Days, assistant attorney general. (Years later, Days would serve as President Bill Clinton's solicitor general.) The administration of then-President Jimmy Carter had decided it had a vested interest in the case and had requested to be present. Both McCree and Days were black.

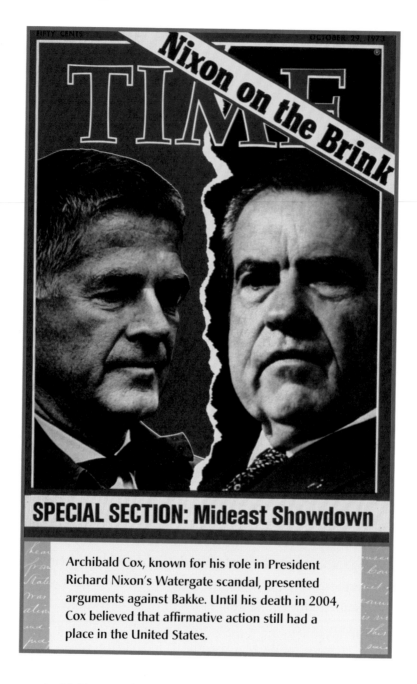

SPECIAL SECTION: Mideast Showdown

Archibald Cox, known for his role in President Richard Nixon's Watergate scandal, presented arguments against Bakke. Until his death in 2004, Cox believed that affirmative action still had a place in the United States.

At 11:00 A.M., the symbolic gavel was rapped, and the nine justices filed in. They took their seats along the mahogany bench, with Chief Justice Warren Burger seated at the center. Justices with seniority sat closest to him, and the justices who had been on the court the least number of years sat on either end of the bench. Normally, lawyers addressing the Supreme Court were given 30 minutes to present their cases. Given the importance of the *Bakke* case, the attorneys had one hour, twice as long. The university's attorneys, however, had to share their time with Wade McCree, who was there to represent the government's support of the school's affirmative action policy.

Since the university had petitioned the court, its attorney, Cox, a tall, rather thin, middle-aged man—one known for his legal intellect—made the first presentation. He appealed to the justices by emphasizing three main points, which he referred to as the "three facts or realities."[132] He claimed that the University of California, Davis, did not make a practice of admitting unqualified candidates to its medical school. In selecting its medical students, Cox argued, Davis was within its rights to use race as a criteria as a tool to correct discrimination against minorities in the past. Cox explained that

> the number of qualified applicants for the nation's professional schools is vastly greater than the number of places available. This is a fact and an inescapable fact. In 1975–76, for example, there were roughly 30,000 qualified applicants for admission to medical school, a much greater number of actual applicants, and there were only about 14,000 places. At Davis, there were 25 applicants for every seat in 1973; in 1974, the ratio had risen to 37 to 1. So the problem is one of selection among qualified applicants, not of ability to gain from a professional education.[133]

Although the admissions program was based, in part, on discrimination, the practice was acceptable, because it discriminated *positively*, on behalf of minorities. Such a policy, argued Cox, did not violate anyone's Fourteenth Amendment rights. He wanted the court to declare the school's dual admissions policy constitutional. As Cox addressed the court, he was poised, professional, and extremely at ease. He "was formal enough to buoy the traditions of the Court, yet familiar enough to participate in a discussion among gentlemen."[134] As a reporter for *Newsweek* would later write, "[Cox] was at his donnish best, fielding questions with confidence, sometimes lecturing the Justices as if they were his Harvard law school students."[135]

 ## "FRIENDS OF THE COURT"

When cases are brought before a court, there are usually two sides, or interested parties. In a civil case, there is a party known as the plaintiff, the person or group filing the suit in the first place, and a second party known as the defendant. Generally, then, the outcome of a civil case falls within the interests of only these two parties. Legal proceedings will render a decision, typically in favor of either the plaintiff or the defendant. One party will win, and the other will lose; one will be satisfied, the other will be disappointed. Sometimes, a judge will make a decision that does not result in a clear winner or loser but will decide partially in favor of both sides. A judge may, in fact, decide in a way that does not favor either side. When Judge Manker made his decision in the *Bakke* case in November 1974, neither party really emerged satisfied with the judge's decision.

Sometimes, however, the outcome of a case has a greater bearing than just the interests of the two parties directly involved. An issue may have such significant ramifications that it will cause changes that impact a much wider circle of parties. The *Bakke* case was certainly such a case. When the case was filed before the California Supreme Court, many of those interested parties made themselves known and became technical participants in the legal proceedings. When an interested party wants to make its interests clear to the court, that party will file a special brief known as an *amicus curiae* (plural, *amici curiae*) brief. (From the Latin, *amicus curiae* means "friend of the court.") Usually, the *amicus curiae*

A DIFFERENT LENS

Following Cox, McCree, speaking for the government, approached the podium. As he spoke, the government attorney argued in opposition to the concept that only institutions with a clear record of discrimination against minorities could legally use racial preferences to right its previous wrongs. McCree also

party will file a brief that supports or reflects the arguments of one of the direct litigant parties, the plaintiff or the defendant. When the *DeFunis v. Odegaard* case was heard before the Washington State Supreme Court, the case had 30 *amici curiae* briefs attached to it. Of those briefs, 22 supported the position taken by the University of Washington Law School. Since *amici curiae* briefs may be filed on behalf of more than one organization, those 22 briefs represented more than 120 interested groups, organizations, and individuals. When the U.S. Supreme Court agreed to hear the case, nearly 60 *amici curiae* briefs were filed—a record number!

Such briefs provide the court with a clearer picture of how important the court's decision will be and how many groups of people might be directly impacted by it. Since such groups have a "stake" in how the court decides, the *amicus curiae* brief gives them an opportunity to have a voice as well.

Perhaps, ironically, the *DeFunis* case produced supporters for both sides that had been united previously on issues regarding civil rights. Whereas the National Council of Jewish Women and the Jewish Rights Council had battled together for equality for America's blacks, they split over the *Bakke* case, with the women's organization supporting the university and the other supporting Bakke. Such was the controversial nature of a case that was based on a white plaintiff claiming his civil rights had been violated.

approached the Fourteenth Amendment with a unique perspective, asking the justices to interpret it through "historical, rather than a strictly literal" lens.[136] The amendment had been created in the aftermath of the Civil War as a protection for the newly freed slaves. The amendment was intended to right the existing wrong of blacks having been held for hundreds of years as slaves. Affirmative action programs, such as the Davis medical school program, were intended to right a long history of another wrong: the denial of minorities to achieve a higher education. In this context, McCree stated, the historical spirit of the Fourteenth Amendment was satisfied by the Davis medical school policy.

Bakke's attorney was the last one to address the justices. As he had from his first court presentation to this one, Reynold Colvin focused much of his address on the issue of his client having been denied admission to the Davis school. He was much less concerned with the greater issue of the policy's constitutionality. His opening words reflected this same strategic point: "I am Allan Bakke's attorney and Allan Bakke is my client." Then, he began telling his client's story, his frustrated pursuit of acceptance into medical school. But the justices were after bigger issues than Bakke's quest to become a doctor. One of the justices, Lewis Powell, finally interrupted him. "We are here," said Powell, "at least I am here, primarily to hear a constitutional argument. You have devoted 20 minutes to belaboring the facts, if I may say so. I would like help, I really would, on the constitutional issues. Would you address that please?"[137]

CONSTITUTIONAL QUESTIONS

Colvin needed no more prompting. He cited the specific laws that he felt were violated by the Davis medical dchool dual admissions policy, including the privileges and immunities portion of the California State Constitution, Title VI of the 1964 Civil Rights Act, and, of course, the Fourteenth Amendment of the U.S. Constitution. The amendment's Equal Protection clause was the main point hammered by Colvin. "As we look at the Fourteenth Amendment . . . the fact of the matter is that . . . it is discrimination on the ground of race which is forbidden."[138]

Bakke's attorney remained firm in his commitment to his client. He stated that it was his legal opinion that the Davis medical school policy had violated Bakke's "right to admission." This statement drew a response from Justice Potter Stewart: "You spoke, Mr. Colvin, of the right to admission. You don't seriously submit that he had a right to be admitted?" Colvin: "That is not Allan Bakke's position. Allan Bakke's position is that he has a right, and that right is not to be discriminated against by reason of his race. And that's what brings Allan Bakke to this court."[139]

As Colvin spoke to the Supreme Court justices, he was presenting one of the most important civil rights cases concerning the American education system since the Supreme Court had heard the *Brown v. Board of Education of Topeka* case in 1954, more than 20 years earlier. The court Colvin was facing did not include a single justice who had been on the court at that time. (The last one, Justice William O. Douglas, had retired just months earlier.) Among the justices, however, was the court's first and only black member, Thurgood Marshall. It had been Marshall, as a lawyer for the NAACP, who had presented on behalf of Brown in 1954.

As a civil rights attorney, Marshall had an unusual interest and a special perspective on the Bakke case. At one point, Marshall asked Colvin if he would be as adamant in his legal position on the Davis medical school's dual policy if the school had set aside only one seat for a disadvantaged person, rather than 16 of every 100. Colvin responded by stating that the number was not the issue with him: "It is the principle of keeping someone out because of his race that is important."[140] During a later exchange, Justice Marshall interrupted Colvin, "You are talking about your client's rights. Don't these underprivileged people have some rights?" Colvin answered, "They certainly have the right to . . ." Then Marshall interrupted, pointedly: "To eat cake."

The first African-American Supreme Court justice,
Thurgood Marshall was once chief counsel for the
NAACP. In the *Regents* case, Marshall aggressively
challenged Bakke's attorney.

Colvin kept his composure and answered the justice, "They have
the right to compete. The right to equal competition."[141]

For two hours, the issue of affirmative action was debated
before the U.S. Supreme Court. Following Colvin's presentation, Cox was allowed time for rebuttal. He was brief and to
the point:

There is no per se rule of color blindness incorporated in the Equal Protection clause [of the Fourteenth Amendment].... The educational, professional, and social purposes accomplished by race conscious admissions programs are compelling objectives, or to put it practically, they are sufficient justification for those losses, those problems that are created by the use of race.... There is no other way of accomplishing those purposes.[142]

Then, the entire proceeding seemed complete. Chief Justice Burger closed the session at two minutes before noon, announcing, "Thank you, gentlemen, the case is submitted."[143] The justices rose immediately from their seats and filed out of the court chamber. The attorneys soon faced a multitude of reporters. With his wife at his side, Archibald Cox answered the questions from the press as coolly as he had presented his case in court. There was a buzz among the crowd and the reporters. Many believed that Cox had simply out-presented Colvin. Bakke's attorney had not followed the lead of several of the justices and their questions, many thought. The thoughts of several who had watched the hearing were mirrored in a comment made by the dean of a prestigious law school who was in attendance, as he joked with some of his professional friends, "Maybe Bakke could appeal the ruling for lack of effective counsel."[144]

Despite the doubts and assurances expressed that day concerning the hearing, everyone would have to wait eight months before the nine justices of the highest court in the land would deliver their decision in this important civil rights case.

10

Bakke's Legacy

The presentation of the *Bakke* case before the U.S. Supreme Court only took a single morning. The justices, however, would make the nation wait eight months before rendering a decision in this landmark case. In their responses, the justices were split into several factions. This became clear the first time the justices were called together following the October 12 case presentation by Colvin, McCree, and Cox. At that meeting, the justices weighed in and a vote was taken to determine where each justice was on the issue. Three justices favored the university and wanted to reverse the decision by the California Supreme Court. Four others supported Bakke's case and wanted to uphold the ban on the Davis medical school's dual admissions policy. An eighth, Justice Harry Blackmun, was not present, but was back in Minnesota, his home state, too sick to respond.

SPLIT DECISION

The last of the justices, Lewis Powell, was not clearly in either camp. Although he, in theory, believed in the use of race in university admissions programs, he did not like the program in place at the University of California, Davis. This meant he wanted to vote on behalf of a portion of the California court's decision and against another part. In addition to these splits, some of the justices favored avoiding a ruling on the constitutionality of the Davis admissions policy, wanting only to interpret the case on the basis of the Civil Rights Act of 1964. This meant that the issue of the Fourteenth Amendment would be ignored. Still others had always thought the constitutionality issue was the most important aspect of their potential decision. Even then, there were serious differences between those who wanted a decision on the constitutionality question regarding the standard the court should use. Without Blackmun, the court did not have a single five-justice majority on any aspect of the case. A month after the case's hearing on October 12, Chief Justice Burger told his colleagues to look at the case individually, discuss its specifics with each other in memos, and stand pat until Justice Blackmun was available to, potentially, break the court's deadlock.

Over the next few months, the justices did consider the case, its specifics, and its ramifications. Memos flew back and forth, as some justices sought to convince their colleagues of their position. In the meantime, Blackmun recovered and returned to the court that spring. He continued to postpone his public view on the case. Then, in May, he wrote a memo of his own, in which he expressed his opinion. Despite being a conservative member of the court, Blackmun stunned his colleagues by announcing his intent to decide in support of those in favor of overturning the California Supreme Court's

On October 12, 1977, hundreds of people lined up outside the Supreme Court building to hear arguments in the *Bakke* case.

decision. The result was a fractured court, with four justices supporting Bakke, another four supporting the university, and the ninth, Justice Powell, splitting his decision between the two. There seemed that no majority decision was possible.

Burger handed the task of writing the court's plurality decision (a plurality exists when no group's vote equals a majority of the court's members) to Powell, because the justice agreed in part with both groups of four justices and their divergent opinions. Powell labored over this important document for weeks. Then, on June 28, 1978, the court's decision was presented publicly. Powell took the microphone on behalf of his colleagues on the court and read the decision. During his presentation, he spoke about the extraordinary attention the case had gained in the media and that the public appeared intensely interested in the case. Then, he gave the court's decision, one that was multilayered, a decision that would lead the *Wall Street Journal* to run a headline describing the results: "The Decision Everybody Won."[145]

Headlines, however, do not tell the complete story. In its details, regarding the *Bakke* case, the decision made by the Supreme Court was as complicated as the subject it was intended to decide. On the surface, the Supreme Court's ruling established the use of race as one of the criteria that may be used in determining the validity of an applicant to a specific school. On the other hand, the court had decided that set quotas, such as the Davis medical school's policy of admitting 16 disadvantaged students per 100 selected, were unacceptable. Powell's primary argument was that Davis's policy had violated Bakke's rights under the Civil Rights Act of 1964. In his opinion, "Racial and ethnic distinctions of any sort are suspect." He did not agree with those who believed that quota systems that "work against the white majority" could ultimately be neutral in nature.[146] Powell went on to give the example of Harvard University's admissions policy. It allowed race to be considered, but the institution also weighed it in conjunction with other important factors, and Harvard did not operate a policy based on quotas.

Powell's plurality opinion was only one of those presented to the public. In all, six of the justices wrote separate opinions. Justice John Paul Stevens wrote an opinion that spoke for the four justices—Stevens, Burger, Potter Stewart, and William Rehnquist—who believed the quota policy at the Davis Medical School was unconstitutional, thus upholding the earlier decision of the California Supreme Court. They expressed the opinion that Bakke's rights had been denied him under Title VI of the Civil Rights Act of 1964, and the decision was that the university, mirroring the California Supreme Court, must allow Bakke to enroll. Justice William Brennan wrote a decision for himself and the other three members of the court—Byron White, Marshall, Harry Blackmun—who favored reversing the California court's ruling by supporting the university's policy. They did not feel that the university's policy and practice had violated the Fourteenth Amendment to the U.S. Constitution. White, Blackmun, and Marshall also wrote individual opinions. Among them, the justices took a full hour making their collective presentations to the media, each explaining his opinion.

IN THE DECISION'S AFTERMATH

Perhaps no one was more pleased with the decision rendered by the U.S. Supreme Court than Allan Bakke himself. Following the Supreme Court's decision, Bakke did not speak in public, but, through his lawyer, expressed his satisfaction with their verdict: "I am pleased and, after five years of waiting, I look forward to entering medical school in the fall."[147] Bakke had always kept a low profile throughout the years the case was working its way through the courts. He had not been seeking a constitutional ruling on the use of affirmative action and had not been speaking on behalf of a wide-ranging group of people with similar complaints. He had been involved in the case that bore his name, because he simply wanted to attend medical school. Given the Court's ruling, he was allowed just that.

On September 25, 1978, Allan Bakke entered the University of California, Davis, medical school. When he arrived at the campus to enroll in classes, Bakke found himself still at center stage. Groups of demonstrators and protesters met him

The attention surrounding Allen Bakke was evident on his first day of medical school at the University of California, Davis. Bakke was assigned plainclothes security officers to protect him from the media frenzy.

and spoke out against him. The court case he had generated and the decision the Supreme Court had made would remain controversial for many years to come. Once Bakke was allowed entrance to the Davis school, though, he fulfilled his dream. Four years later, in 1982, Bakke graduated with his medical degree. He then quietly left California to work on his internship at the Mayo Clinic in Minnesota, his home state.

As for the University of California, Davis, School of Medicine, officials changed the admissions policy to fall into line with the U.S. Supreme Court's decision. They altered the minority admissions program, establishing a ratings system for applicants based on an accumulation of points. Students received points for their grades and test scores, as well as points according to their race. In time, the California Superior Court rendered yet another important decision concerning the *Bakke* case. The court ordered the University of California to pay Bakke's legal fees, which had climbed to more than $180,000.

In the years that followed the *Bakke* decision, the use of affirmative action in assessing applications for admission in America's colleges and universities has not disappeared. Although schools began abandoning quota systems by the late 1970s, the use of race as one of the criteria considered for admissions went under a retooling. After Justice Powell had used the Harvard University system as a prime example of how to use race as an admissions criteria, many university programs shifted toward this more subjective approach.

In other arenas of American public life, affirmative action remained viable. During the year after the *Bakke* decision, the Supreme Court decided the case *United Steelworkers v. Weber* that affirmed the right of a private employer to use affirmative action. In 1980, the Supreme Court again ruled in support of another affirmative action program in the case of *Fullilove v. Klutznick*, a case centered on a federal program that reserved for minority companies 10 percent of public works funds budgeted for such infrastructure items as bridges and highways. The justification for the court was that the program attempted to correct a previous wrong that had favored white-owned

On Allen Bakke's first day of medical school, affirmative action supporters protest the Supreme Court's decision of his case. The issue of affirmative action is still debated today.

companies over minority businesses. In the 1980s, President Ronald Reagan, a conservative Republican, supported the elimination of all affirmative action programs.

All such programs were not ended, though. The court continued to support some programs based on their structure, intent, purpose, and design to correct past wrongs. During the 1990s, for example, President Bill Clinton sought to have affirmative action programs reworked to make them more acceptable. By 1995, the U.S. Supreme Court was deciding affirmative action cases on the basis of first establishing a "compelling government interest."[148] Following the Supreme Court decision in *Adarand v. Pena*, new guidelines concerning affirmative action programs were established for the government. These guidelines would require government affirmative action programs, to do the following:

1. Involve temporary measures, with a definite ending point
2. Target actual past discrimination against a specific minority group, either by a governmental agency or by the people within the jurisdiction in question, and
3. Be narrowly focused to achieve a specific result.[149]

Once the *Adarand* decision was established, it became more difficult to justify future affirmative action programs.

As for California, where the *Bakke* case had originated back in the 1970s, important steps were taken during the mid-1990s in opposition to affirmative action. In July 1995, the Regents of the University of California closed down all preferential affirmative action admissions policies and programs within the university system. The following year, in December, California voters passed Proposition 209, which effectively ended all affirmative action programs within the state associated with employment, education, and public contracts.

Today, affirmative action programs must jump a variety of hurdles and meet almost endless legal criteria to be accepted in the business world, in academic settings, or as part of a government program. Although the goal of such programs—to right past wrongs and give minorities new opportunities—has never gone away, Americans still struggle in their support of any system based on preference or bias simply because of one's race. At the heart of the continuing debate surrounding affirmative action programs are a series of overarching questions: What does this country owe its minority populations? Is a system that is advantageous to one and disadvantageous to another truly fair? How does the American promise of justice and equality for all play out on a stage filled with so many different types of actors, each having his or her own talents, aspirations, and—as was the case for aerospace engineer Allan Bakke—dreams that long to touch reality. In asking and considering such questions, Americans might have to return to the words of Thomas Jefferson— "all men are created equal"—and ask themselves how the words from that eighteenth-century phrase should be considered in twenty-first-century America.

Chronology

1964　Congress passes the Civil Rights Act, which includes Title VI, banning discrimination on the basis of race, color, sex, or national origin.

1970　University of California, Davis, School of Medicine establishes an affirmative action admissions program

Timeline

1970
University of California, Davis, School of Medicine establishes an affirmative action admissions program based on a dual admissions policy and a quota system.

May 1973
Bakke is rejected for admission at Davis.

April 1974
Allan Bakke is rejected again for admission to Davis.

November 1974
Judge sets aside the Davis dual admissions policy but decides not to force the university to admit Bakke.

1970

1974

1972
Allan Bakke begins sending out applications to medical schools, including the University of California, Davis.

September 1973
Bakke is rejected for early admission to Davis.

June 1974
Bakke files a suit in Yolo County, California, Superior Court.

based on a dual admissions policy and a quota system.

April 1971   Washington Superior Court rules on behalf of Marco DeFunis and against the University of Washington Law School's affirmative action policy for admissions.

May 1972   Washington State Supreme Court overturns the earlier DeFunis decision and declares the University of Washington Law School's admissions policy legal.

August 1972   DeFunis files *writ of certiorari* to the U.S. Supreme Court for his case to be heard.

September 1976
California Supreme Court affirms lower court decision and orders Bakke admitted to the University of California.

December 1976
Regents of the University of California appeal to the U.S. Supreme Court.

October 12, 1977
Oral arguments are presented by both sides in the Bakke case.

September 25, 1978
Allan Bakke enters the University of California, Davis, School of Medicine. 1982.

1976   **1982**

1975
Regents of the University of California appeal the lower court decision to the California Supreme Court.

June 28, 1978
U.S. Supreme Court announces its decision in *Regents of the University of California v. Bakke.*

1982
Bakke graduates from medical school.

	That same month, the University of Washington allows DeFunis to enroll while the Court decides whether to hear his case.
1972	Allan Bakke, a 32-year-old California aerospace engineer begins sending out applications to medical schools, including the University of California, Davis.
May 1973	Bakke is rejected for admission at Davis.
August 3, 1973	Bakke meets with University of California, Davis, medical school admissions officer Peter Storandt, who describes the dual admissions policy of the medical school.
September 1973	Bakke is rejected for early admission to Davis.
April 23, 1974	U.S. Supreme Court dismisses *DeFunis* case.
April 1974	Allan Bakke is rejected again for admission to Davis.
June 1974	Bakke files a lawsuit in Yolo County, California, Superior Court against Davis, based on the school's preferential policy.
November 1974	Judge sets aside the Davis dual admissions policy but decides not to force the university to admit Bakke.
May 1975	Regents of the University of California appeal the lower court decision to the California Supreme Court.
September 1976	California Supreme Court affirms lower court decision and orders Bakke admitted to the University of California, Davis, School of Medicine.
December 1976	Regents of the University of California appeal to the U.S. Supreme Court. The high court places a stay on admitting Bakke to Davis until a decision is made.

February 22, 1977	U.S. Supreme Court grants *certiorari* and agrees to hear the *Bakke* case during its fall session.
June 1977	University attorneys file a brief before the U.S. Supreme Court.
August 1977	Reynold Colvin, Bakke's attorney, files a brief in response.
October 12, 1977	Oral arguments are presented by both sides in the Bakke case.
June 28, 1978	U.S. Supreme Court announces its decision in *Regents of the University of California v. Bakke.*
September 25, 1978	Allan Bakke enters the University of California, Davis, School of Medicine.
1979	Supreme Court decides the case *United Steelworkers v. Weber,* which affirms the right of a private employer to use affirmative action.
1980	Supreme Court rules in support of affirmative action program through *Fullilove v. Klutznick.*
1982	Bakke graduates from medical school.
June 1995	U.S. Supreme Court decides *Adarand v. Pena* in support of affirmative action programs on the basis of a "compelling government interest."
July 1995	Regents of University of California end all affirmative action admissions programs within the university system.
November 1996	California voters approve Proposition 209, which ends all state affirmative action programs associated with employment, education, and public contracts.

Notes

Chapter 1

1. Quoted in Joel Dreyfuss and Charles Lawrence III, *The Bakke Case: The Politics of Inequality*. New York: Harcourt Brace Jovanovich, 1979, p. 11.
2. Ibid., p. 4
3. Ibid.
4. Ibid.
5. Ibid., p. 16.
6. Ibid., p. 12.
7. Ibid., p. 11.
8. Ibid., p. 13.
9. Ibid., p. 16.
10. Ibid., p. 23.
11. Ibid., p. 17.
12. Ibid., p. 19.
13. Ibid.
14. Ibid., p. 23.
15. Ibid., p. 5.
16. Quoted in Darlene Clark Hine, *The African-American Odyssey*. Upper Saddle River, NJ: Prentice Hall, 2005, p. 50.
17. Ibid.
18. Ibid., p. 51.
19. Ibid.
20. Ibid., p. 53.
21. Ibid., p. 54.
22. Quoted in Benjamin Quarles, *The Negro in the Making of America*, rev. ed. New York: Collier, 1969, pp. 69–70.
23. Quoted in Tim McNeese, *The Rise and Fall of American Slavery: Freedom Denied, Freedom Gained*. Berkeley Heights, NJ: Enslow, 2004, p. 57.
24. Ibid., p. 58.
25. Quoted in Hine, *The African-American Odyssey*, p. 104.
26. Ibid.
27. Ibid.

Chapter 2

28. Quoted in J. F. Watts, *The Irish Americans*. New York: Chelsea House, 1988, p. 40.
29. Ibid., p. 41.
30. Ibid., p. 43.
31. Quoted in Marjorie R. Fallows, *Irish Americans: Identity and Assimilation*. Englewood Cliffs, NJ: Prentice-Hall, 1979, p. 27.
32. Quoted in Watts, *The Irish Americans,* p. 43.
33. Quoted in Fallows, *Irish Americans,* p. 27.
34. Ibid., p. 56.
35. Ibid., p. 33.
36. Quoted in David Goldfield, *The American Journey: A History of the United States*, 3rd ed. Upper Saddle River, NJ: Prentice Hall, 2004, p. 585.
37. Ibid.

38. Quoted in James Kirby Martin, *A Concise History of America and Its People.* New York: HarperCollins College Publishers, 1995, p. 455.
39. Ibid.
40. Quoted in William Daley, *The Chinese Americans.* New York: Chelsea House, 1987, p. 46.

Chapter 3
41. Quoted in Hine, *The African-American Odyssey*, p. 277.
42. Ibid., p. 298.
43. Quoted in Robert J. Cottroll, Raymond T. Diamond, and Leland B. Ware, *Brown v. Board of Education: Caste, Culture, and the Constitution.* Lawrence: University Press of Kansas, 2003, p. 55.
44. Ibid., p. 132.

Chapter 4
45. Quoted in Howard Ball, *The Bakke Case: Race, Education, and Affirmative Action.* Lawrence: University Press of Kansas, 2000, p. 47.
46. Quoted in J. Harvie Wilkinson, *From Brown to Bakke: The Supreme Court and School Integration, 1954-1978.* New York: Oxford University Press, 1979, p. 254.
47. Ibid.
48. Ibid.
49. Quoted in Dreyfuss and Lawrence, *The Bakke Case,* p. 13.
50. Ibid., p. 16.
51. Quoted in Ball, *The Bakke Case,* p. 47.
52. Quoted in Dreyfuss and Lawrence, *The Bakke Case,* p. 16.
53. Ibid.
54. Ibid., p. 17.
55. Ibid.
56. Ibid.
57. Ibid., p. 18.
58. Ibid., p. 17.
59. Ibid., p. 18.
60. Ibid.
61. Quoted in Ball, *The Bakke Case,* p. 50.

Chapter 5
62. Quoted in Ball, *The Bakke Case,* p. 50.
63. Quoted in Dreyfuss and Lawrence, *The Bakke Case*, p. 21.
64. Ibid.
65. Ibid., p. 22.
66. Ibid.
67. Ibid.
68. Ibid.
69. Ibid.
70. Ibid.
71. Ibid., p. 23.
72. Ibid., p. 25.
73. Ibid.
74. Ibid., p. 26.
75. Ibid., p. 28.
76. Ibid.
77. Ibid.
78. Ibid.
79. Ibid., p. 29.
80. Ibid.

Chapter 6
81. Dreyfuss and Lawrence, *The Bakke Case*, p. 33.
82. Ibid.
83. Ibid., p. 34.
84. Ibid., p. 35.

85. Quoted in Wilkinson, *From Brown to Bakke*, p. 257.

86. Ibid.

87. Quoted in Rebecca Stefoff, *The Bakke Case: Challenging Affirmative Action*. New York: Marshall Cavendish, 2006, p. 56.

88. Ibid., p. 77.

89. Ibid., p. 57.

90. Ibid., p. 58.

91. Ibid.

92. Ibid., p. 57.

93. Quoted in Wilkinson, *From Brown to Bakke*, p. 257.

94. Quoted in Stefoff, *The Bakke Case*, p. 57.

95. Quoted in Dreyfuss and Lawrence, *The Bakke Case*, p. 36.

Chapter 7

96. Quoted in Dreyfuss and Lawrence, *The Bakke Case*, p. 36.

97. Ibid., p. 37.

98. Ibid.

99. Ibid.

100. Ibid., pp. 37–38.

101. Ibid., p. 38.

102. Ibid., p. 39.

103. Ibid., p. 40.

104. Ibid.

105. Ibid., p. 41.

106. Ibid., p. 42.

107. Ibid.

108. Ibid., p. 45.

109. Ibid., p. 48.

110. Ibid., p. 49.

111. Ibid., p. 50.

112. Ibid., p. 51.

113. Ibid.

114. Ibid.

115. Ibid., p. 59.

Chapter 8

116. Quoted in Dreyfuss and Lawrence, *The Bakke Case*, p. 62.

117. Quoted in Stefoff, *The Bakke Case*, p. 78.

118. Quoted in Dreyfuss and Lawrence, *The Bakke Case*, p. 63.

119. Ibid., p. 64.

120. Quoted in Stefoff, *The Bakke Case*, p. 78.

121. Quoted in Dreyfuss and Lawrence, *The Bakke Case*, p. 65.

122. Ibid., p. 68.

123. Ibid., p. 69.

124. Ibid., p. 70.

125. Ibid.

126. Ibid., p. 74.

127. Ibid., p. 75.

128. Ibid., p. 73.

Chapter 9

129. Quoted in Wilkinson, *From Brown to Bakke*, p. 259.

130. Ibid.

131. Quoted in Dreyfuss and Lawrence, *The Bakke Case*, p. 174.

132. Ibid., p. 179.

133. Ibid.

134. Ibid., p. 176.

135. Quoted in Wilkinson, *From Brown to Bakke*, p. 261.

136. Quoted in Stefoff, *The Bakke Case*, p. 95.

137. Ibid., p. 94, and Susan Banfield, *The Bakke Case: Quotas in College Admissions*. Springfield, NJ: Enslow, 1998, p. 80.

138. Quoted in Banfield, *The Bakke Case*, pp. 80–81.

139. Quoted in Dreyfuss and Lawrence, *The Bakke Case*, pp. 196–197.

140. Quoted in Stefoff, *The Bakke Case*, p. 96.

141. Quoted in Wilkinson, *From Brown to Bakke*, p. 262.

142. Quoted in Dreyfuss and Lawrence, *The Bakke Case*, p. 200.

143. Quoted in Stefoff, *The Bakke Case*, p. 96.

144. Quoted in Dreyfuss and Lawrence, *The Bakke Case*, p. 201.

Chapter 10

145. Quoted in Stefoff, *The Bakke Case*, p. 102.

146. Quoted in Banfield, *The Bakke Case*, p. 87.

147. Quoted in Stefoff, *The Bakke Case*, p. 106.

148. Quoted in Banfield, *The Bakke Case*, p. 105.

149. Ibid., p. 106.

Glossary

affidavit a written statement made under oath.

affirmative action an effort to improve the rights and opportunities of disadvantaged people to make up for past bad treatment.

amicus curiae someone not involved in a case who advises the court through a report on a subject in which they are an expert.

appeal to take a court case to a higher court for review.

burden of proof The duty to prove disputed facts.

catalyst someone or something that causes or speeds up change.

class action suit a legal device that allows a group of people with a common complaint to join together as plaintiffs in a single lawsuit.

dissent a difference of opinion.

indentured servant a person who is bound to work for someone else for a fixed number of years in exchange for shelter or free passage to another country.

Jim Crow the laws that arose in the South after the Civil War that allowed discrimination against African Americans to continue.

litigant a person who is involved in a lawsuit.

moot of no legal significance, when events have placed a matter beyond the reach of the law.

plaintiff the person who initiates a lawsuit by filing a complaint.

precedent something that may serve as an example or rule to be followed in the future.

ratify to approve and make valid.

regent a member of governing board.

writ of certiorari an order issued by the Supreme Court demanding that a case be brought before it from a lower court for review.

Bibliography

Ball, Howard. *The Bakke Case: Race, Education, and Affirmative Action*. Lawrence: University Press of Kansas, 2000.

Cottroll, Robert J., Raymond T. Diamond, and Leland B. Ware. *Brown v. Board of Education: Caste, Culture, and the Constitution*. Lawrence: University Press of Kansas, 2003.

Cunningham, Noble. *In Pursuit of Reason: The Life of Thomas Jefferson*. Baton Rouge: Louisiana State University Press, 1987.

Daley, William. *The Chinese Americans*. New York: Chelsea House, 1987.

Dreyfuss, Joel, and Charles Lawrence III. *The Bakke Case: The Politics of Inequality*. New York: Harcourt Brace Jovanovich, 1979.

Fallows, Marjorie R. *Irish Americans: Identity and Assimilation*. Englewood Cliffs, NJ: Prentice-Hall, 1979.

Goldfield, David. *The American Journey: A History of the United States*, 3rd ed. Upper Saddle River, NJ: Prentice Hall, 2004.

Hine, Darlene Clark. *The African-American Odyssey*. Upper Saddle River, NJ: Prentice Hall, 2005.

Johnson, James E. *The Irish in America*. Minneapolis, MN: Lerner Publications, 1981.

Martin, James Kirby. *A Concise History of America and Its People*. New York: HarperCollins College, 1995.

McNeese, Tim. *The Rise and Fall of American Slavery: Freedom Denied, Freedom Gained*. Berkeley Heights, NJ: Enslow, 2004.

Quarles, Benjamin. *The Negro in the Making of America*, rev. ed. New York: Collier, 1969.

Simmons, Ron. *Affirmative Action: Conflict and Change in Higher Education After Bakke*. Cambridge, MA: Schenkman, 1982.

Stefoff, Rebecca. *The Bakke Case: Challenging Affirmative Action*. New York: Marshall Cavendish, 2006.

Watts, J. F. *The Irish Americans*. New York: Chelsea House, 1988.

Wilkinson, J. Harvie. *From Brown to Bakke: The Supreme Court and School Integration, 1954–1978*. New York: Oxford University Press, 1979.

Further Reading

Banfield, Susan. *The Bakke Case: Quotas in College Admissions.*
  Springfield, NJ: Enslow, 1998.

Maizilli, Alan. *Affirmative Action.* New York: Chelsea House
  Publishers, 2004.

McNeese, Tim. *Plessy v. Ferguson.* New York: Chelsea House
  Publlishers, 2006.McPherson, Stephanie Sammartino. *The Bakke
  Case and the Affirmative Action Debate.* Berkeley Heights, NJ:
  Enslow, 2005.

Schultz, David. *Encyclopedia of the Supreme Court.* New York:
  Facts on File, 2005.

Wagner, Heather Lehr. *The Supreme Court.* New York: Chelsea House
  Publishers, 2007.

Web sites

www.brownat50.org/brownCases/PostBrownCases/bakke1978.htm
www.debatingracialpreference.org/BAKKE-Facts.htm
www.landmarkcases.org/bakke/pdf/regents_of_ca_v_bakke.pdf
www.oyez.org/oyez/resource/case/324

Picture Credits

Index

About the Author

Tim McNeese is an associate professor of history at York College in York, Nebraska, where he is in his fifteenth year of college instruction. Professor McNeese earned his Associate of Arts degree from York College, a Bachelor of Arts in history and political science from Harding University, and a Master of Arts in history from Southwest Missouri State University. He taught social studies, English, and journalism in public school for 16 years. A prolific author of books for elementary, middle- and high-school, and college readers, McNeese has published more than 80 books and educational materials over the past 20 years, on subjects from Marco Polo to the siege of the Alamo. His writing earned him a citation in the library reference work, *Something about the Author*. In 2005, his textbook *Political Revolutions of the 18th, 19th, and 20th Centuries* was published. Professor McNeese served as a consulting historian for the History Channel program, "Risk Takers, History Makers: John Wesley Powell and the Grand Canyon." He is a consulting contributor to the 2007 edition of *The World Book Encyclopedia*. His wife, Beverly, is an assistant professor of English at York College, and they have two children, Noah and Summer, and two grandchildren, Ethan and Adrianna. Readers are encouraged to contact Professor McNeese at tdmcneese@york.edu.